COMMON CORE

UNIT BY UNIT

COMMON
CORE
UNIT BY UNIT

5 Critical Moves
for Implementing the Reading Standards Across the Curriculum

Cheryl Becker Dobbertin

Foreword by **Carol Ann Tomlinson**

HEINEMANN
Portsmouth, NH

Heinemann
361 Hanover Street
Portsmouth, NH 03801–3912
www.heinemann.com

Offices and agents throughout the world

The author and publisher wish to thank those who have generously given permission to reprint borrowed material:

Excerpts from the Common Core State Standards © Copyright 2010. National Governors Association Center for Best Practices and Council of Chief State School Officers. All rights reserved.

Learning Standards for Social Studies © Copyright 1996. New York State Education Department. Used with permission.

Next Generation Science Standards is a registered trademark of Achieve. Neither Achieve nor the lead states and partners that developed the Next Generation Science Standards was involved in the production of, and does not endorse, this product.

Library of Congress Cataloging-in-Publication Data
Dobbertin, Cheryl Becker.
    Common core, unit by unit : 5 critical moves for implementing the reading standards across the curriculum / Cheryl Becker Dobbertin.
        pages cm.
    ISBN 978-0-325-04885-7
    1. Language arts—Standards—United States.   2. Reading—United States.   I. Title.
    LB1576.D582 2013
    372.6—dc23   2013009195

Editor: Samantha Bennett
Production: Hilary Zusman
Cover and interior designs: Monica Ann Crigler
Typesetter: Gina Poirier Design
Manufacturing: Steve Bernier

Printed in the United States of America on acid-free paper
17 16 15 14 13 VP 1 2 3 4 5

— DEDICATION —

To Tim, who always believes that I can do whatever it is.
To Jessica, Andrew, Erin, and Matthew, whose mom has been
pretty busy teaching teachers about teaching.

I love you guys.

— CONTENTS —

Foreword by Carol Ann Tomlinson *ix*
Acknowledgments *xiii*

INTRODUCTION WHY PLAN DIFFERENTLY FOR THE COMMON CORE? *xv*
 › Josh Needs to Read Better *xv*
 › Teaching Josh Means Action Planning *xvi*
 › Why Plan Differently? *xvi*
   ◆ Commit to Articulating Long-Range Plans *xvii*
   ◆ Envision Contextualized Content *xviii*
   ◆ Develop Student-Shared Goals *xviii*
   ◆ Select Strategies That Build Understanding *xix*
   ◆ Differentiate Purposefully *xix*
 › How to Read This "How To" Book *xx*

CHAPTER 1 ARTICULATE LONG-RANGE PLANS *1*
 › Seeing the Need to Change *1*
 › Change at Both the Classroom and System Level *3*
 › Surface Change vs. Substantive Change *5*
 › The Steps in Long-Range Planning *11*
   ◆ Up Front: Envisioning an Immediately Relevant Context and Product *12*
   ◆ Up Front: Selecting a Variety of Resources to Meet All Students' Needs *14*
   ◆ Up Front: Strategizing to Match the Plans to Actual Kids *15*
   ◆ Implementing: Monitoring Along the Way *16*
   ◆ The Final Stage: Reflecting *16*
 › Keys to Help You Make This Critical Move *17*

CHAPTER 2 ENVISION CONTEXTUALIZED CONTENT *18*
 › How Will Andrew Respond? *18*
 › Walking a Mile in Boo Radley's Shoes *19*
 › Planning a Compelling Context for Reading *20*
 › Using Intriguing Questions to Test Theories *22*
 › Investigating Local Issues *25*
 › Exploring Local History *27*
 › Examining Ideas from Multiple Perspectives *29*

› Analyzing Mentor Texts   *30*
› The Challenge of Context plus Complexity   *32*
› Finding Complex Yet Compelling Texts   *35*
› Keys to Help You Make This Critical Move   *37*

CHAPTER 3   DEVELOP STUDENT-SHARED GOALS   *38*

› How Historians Read   *38*
› Where Student-Shared Learning Targets Come From   *39*
› Creating and Organizing a Variety of Targets   *42*
› Creating Targets and Matched Assessments   *43*
› Daily Structures to Ensure That Students Understand and Use the Targets   *44*
› Moving Beyond Tracking   *46*
› The Impact of Clear Targets and Assessments on Student Learning   *47*
› Keys to Help You Make This Critical Move   *48*

CHAPTER 4   SELECT STRATEGIES THAT BUILD UNDERSTANDING   *50*

› The Problem with Assigning and Assessing   *51*
› Shifting to Prepare-Process-Assess   *52*
› Foundational Strategies: Close Reading and Strategic Questioning   *55*
› Preparing Students for Close Reading   *56*
› A Close Look at Close Reading   *57*
› Strategies That Help Students Dig Even Deeper   *59*
› Assessing Students' Reading Work   *64*
› Designing Close-Reading Lessons   *65*
› Designing Strategic Questions   *68*
› Selecting Additional Processing Strategies   *70*
› Keys to Help You Make This Critical Move   *72*
› Reproducible Classroom Tools   *73*

CHAPTER 5   PURPOSEFULLY DIFFERENTIATE   *105*

› Purposefully Meeting Students' Readiness Needs   *106*
› Purposeful Pre-assessment   *109*
› An Essential Approach: Tiered Processing Activities   *110*
› The Power of Choice   *114*
› Choice by Learning Preference   *117*
› It's Planning Time Spent Now or Later   *122*
› Keys to Help You Make This Critical Move   *123*

PARTING THOUGHTS   *124*

── FOREWORD ──

In my early days at the University of Virginia, one of my roles was to "supervise" student teachers in their field placements. One of the novice teachers with whom I worked (Julie will do for a name) was struggling mightily with the urban middle schoolers in her classes. Her early instincts about the students were not helpful, and the kids—as kids are prone to do—saw her as easy bait. When they acted out, she generally redoubled her efforts in whatever direction was already not working. Daily, the scene was one that many teachers have nightmares about. Five periods a day, she tried to teach, and rarely was there a student focused on anything remotely associated with learning.

Truth be told, I was about as raw at my job as Julie was at hers. I knew how to teach well enough, but really had no idea how to help someone else learn. I tried varied approaches to help her reign in the chaos, but short of being in the room with her all day every day, I struggled to find clear, economical, and practical ways to help her think about, plan for, and carry out instruction. Everything was wrong. She was afraid of the students, and was coming to dislike them. Her approach to curriculum was flat and formulaic. Her plans for instruction pivoted around worksheets which grew exponentially as things veered out of control, and, of course, contributed to all things negative in Julie's classes. Her sense of classroom leadership and management was absent.

One of many approaches to helping her re-direct her thinking seemed practical and promising to me. I arranged to have her visit three teachers in her school. Their personalities were quite different, but all of them were real McCoy master teachers. Watching them work was, for me, like looking at art or listening to a symphony or seeing a prime athlete perform. Julie would, I reasoned, have a chance to see quality teaching in action in a context that allowed her space and time for reflection. The visits would provide her with models of effective teaching. She could see in action the elements I was talking with her about and the elements would be concrete, visible. Julie seemed happy with the idea, certainly in part because during the visits she'd be spared the gut-wrenching agony of being "in charge of" a class.

One night, well after midnight, my phone rang. I was sleeping so soundly that it took me a bit to figure out who was calling, or what planet we were on for that matter. Getting situated in a context was made more difficult because the person on the other end of the line was sobbing and her speech was difficult to interpret. "I can't be a teacher anymore," she choked. "I called to tell you I need to drop out of the teacher ed. program."

As I struggled to orient myself and to find the right words to encourage Julie, I tried to buy a little time by asking her a question. "Did you have a chance to visit the classes we talked about?"

"Yes," she choked. "I went to all of them."

"What did you come away thinking about?" I asked, sleep still making my voice clumsy.

Her response was in the form of an extended and desperate wail. "I came away thinking they know how to teach, and if I knew whatever it is they know, I'd be a good teacher, too…"

Once I got past being overcome by my own incompetence, I've revisited that moment countless times. How often have I asked students to do something they had no idea how to do (analyze an argument, turn the short story into a play, teach the class on a specified topic…) and assumed that my explaining the task or their examination of a competent example constituted appropriate instruction?

Why is it so easy to forget that teaching is not telling—or even showing? Why don't we readily operate from the knowledge that effective teaching is coaching each kid from his or her starting point, mentoring individual growth, through a sequence of identifiable steps? Why aren't we repelled at the thought that we pronounce a student to be inadequate when he or she doesn't perform to our expectations after our teaching failed to lift those students to our expectations? And why aren't we uncomfortable in telling some students they are "smart" because they met our expectations by showing us what they already knew how to do, rather than because they struggled to grow?

There are many possible answers to those questions, most of them complex, and many of them having to do with the habitual nature of how we "do school." No doubt a contributor to our oddly formed thinking about teaching and learning is the sort of blind-man-figuring-out-the-elephant approach through which many of us develop as teachers.

Or maybe I'm just talking about myself. You decide.

I had no formal mentoring as a young teacher—or as a teacher at any stage, for that matter. On many days, I knew something wasn't working in my classes because some or many of my students weren't psyched about learning or because they simply weren't learning. I had little idea what the something was or how to go about changing things for the better. On some days, teaching was a dream. The kids were electric with enthusiasm. Aha moments were audible or visible. I couldn't really have told you why. Some days I was told by superordinates that my teaching was good. I recall clearly wishing I knew what that meant. There was a checklist, of course, but it did nothing to move me past my surface-level understanding of my craft.

We aren't helpless as teachers. I read about teaching hungrily and some of the authors I read became critical friends, challenging and extending my beliefs and practices—often re-shaping them significantly. And I gravitated toward colleagues who were reflective practitioners and who would share their ideas and energies with me, and they helped me grow considerably in my sense of what my profession and practice meant and what they could be.

In the end, however, I didn't really understand my work with the kind of coherence that should characterize a professional in any field until I left my first life as a public school teacher after twenty-one years to join a university faculty. Only then did I discover the science of teaching. Only then did I find the vocabulary that gave precision to the work I had been doing for over two decades. Only then did I have the opportunity to engage in extended and sometimes heated conversations about the implications of how we approach teaching for kids, schools, society, and our profession.

I am exhilarated by teaching—always have been—even on the days when I've been sure, like Julie, that I'd never be a decent teacher and should bow out before I embarrassed myself any further. On the good days, I felt transcendent. On both, I understood that there was a direct connection between quality teaching and personal development.

I'm sad, though, that it took me so long to develop a framework for thinking about teaching in a way that reflected the full knowledge of my profession. I'm sad that I didn't very fully understand the symbiotic relationship between classroom environment and quality of curriculum, between teacher clarity about goals and student autonomy, between style of classroom management and the nature of student thought. I'm sad that no one ever sat down with me in my classroom and said, "Can you tell me why you're doing this in this way?" I'm sorry I didn't have a coach who straightforwardly said to me, "Of course teaching will consume you. How else do you think you'll be ready for the challenge of 150 young lives every day?"

And I'm sorry I didn't have this book to read in the first two decades of my teaching life. It speaks in a clear, no frills voice. It provides a framework for thinking about curriculum that makes the work as creative for me as I want curriculum to be for my students. It presents a toolkit of instructional approaches that scaffold a progression of student thinking. It casts attention to student differences as the inescapable next step of formative assessment, as the core of planning for student success rather than as an extra. It provides a vocabulary that helps me think more crisply and precisely about my work, a vocabulary that enables me to have progressive aspirations for myself and for my students. It reflects both the humanity and the science of stellar teaching. And it reminds me that while there are no shortcuts to excellent teaching, the investment in quality, as always, is a wise one.

In reading this book, I felt as though I had the sort of classroom coach and mentor I didn't even know to wish for as a public school teacher. I'll take that. Better late than never.

—Carol Ann Tomlinson

ACKNOWLEDGMENTS

After my first meeting with the Northeast Regional Staff of Expeditionary Learning six years ago, I called my husband, slightly tearful, and said, "I think I finally found my people." To the tremendously talented, committed, and passionate educators of the Expeditionary Learning network, thank you. You've changed my life. To the Powerful Women, it's an amazing feeling to belong. To Suzanne Nathan Plaut, my fellow ninja, I'd rather be in the fetal position under a desk with you more than any other. Thank you, Samantha Bennett, thank you for always making even the hardest feedback feel congratulatory. Thank you to my parents for nurturing my little light. Finally, thank you to my own best teacher ever, Sue Meier. You told the class I was an author. I believed you.

— INTRODUCTION —

WHY PLAN DIFFERENTLY FOR THE COMMON CORE?

Josh Needs to Read Better

Josh was my summer school student. He was seventeen years old, gangly-tall, and worried about graduating from high school. Josh had failed the requisite New York State Regents exam in English/Language Arts, which most New York kids take at the end of their junior year. He was a special education student, so he qualified for the "safety net" of needing to get only fifty-five percent to be granted credit for the exam. After just a few days of watching him in class and looking at his work, it became pretty clear to me why Josh did not earn the fifty-five he needed on his first attempt at the exam. His reading was laboriously slow, and he was hyper-focused on highlighting information that he thought would help him answer questions. His writing was limited because his reading was limited. He did not think much about the text, so he didn't have a lot to say about it.

Josh was a friendly, open kid and we talked a lot. One day, as we were conferencing about his work, I said something along the lines of, "Yeah, Josh, I can see why you're worried about passing the test. Reading is super hard for you, huh?" There was just a moment of silence, and then Josh blurted out, "Thank God someone finally noticed!"

I so strongly remember this interaction with Josh because it made me deeply angry. Of *course* Josh's teachers, and likely his parents, had noticed over the years that he wasn't reading well. But clearly no one had mentioned it to Josh, probably from some misplaced sense of protecting him. This poor kid traveled through school, year after year, wondering who was going to notice his reading problem. He wondered who was going to help fix it. He must have wondered if people had just given up on him.

The Common Core State Standards for English Language Arts and Literacy in History/Social Studies, Science, and Technical Subjects ("the Standards") are changing reading instruction for all kids. But I am particularly hopeful that as teachers and leaders dig into planning to implement the new Standards, and, along with them the accompanying shifts in instruction, that school will change especially for kids like Josh. Josh didn't need a "program" or technological aids to improve his reading, which was good because I didn't have those to offer him anyway. What Josh needed in order to finally improve his reading skills was:

> › carefully planned units, designed around motivating reasons to read and re-read all kinds of texts (even the ones he initially thought were way too hard)
> › clarity about what reading was supposed to look like and be like in his head
> › reasons and methods to change his "look for the answer" mentality
> › the essential scaffolds he needed that didn't exempt him from the hard work he needed to do.

We read and thought and talked and wrote like crazy for the six weeks I had him in summer school.

Josh ended up getting a sixty-five percent when he retook the English Regents exam at the end of the summer. I could not wait to call him and let him know that he'd achieved his goal. "Sixty-five!" he said, delighted. "That's what *regular* ed kids get on the Regents exam!" Josh had met his own internal benchmark of "normal," a grade that most students must earn to pass the test. Never was a sixty-five more celebrated!

Teaching Josh Means Action Planning

I don't teach high school anymore but I do teach teachers, both as a part-time college instructor and through professional development provided to schools and school districts. When I tell the story of Josh, many teachers nod and smile a little wistfully. Apparently the experience of discovering a student who is feeling "unnoticed" is not uncommon in the life of an educator. This book is my attempt to help educators plan engaging, literacy-focused curriculum that opens the door for every student to get noticed, every day. This kind of teaching cannot be bought in a package and is surely not the result of simply putting new standards on old lessons. I recognize the work that is ahead for teachers and kids, and I know that many of them are wrestling with the idea of working even harder than they already do. But the real change will come, not through harder work but through smarter work—carefully articulating unit plans that give kids reasons to read, carefully selecting standards-aligned strategies, differentiating carefully and purposefully, and reflecting in order to make the right next choices.

Why Plan Differently?

The basic container of content—in any class or subject—is a unit, a chunk of instruction that has a launch, or beginning that sets kids up to learn; a middle, in which teachers help students acquire new knowledge, learn or further develop their skills, and deepen their understanding of concepts; and an end, which is often a summative assessment. Many teachers know that good unit design actually begins at the end, by developing a standards-aligned assessment, and then planning the lessons that will teach the students the knowledge, skills, and understandings that will be assessed—the opposite of the order in which they will be taught. Unit planning takes time, focus, and diligence. It's hard work.

The Common Core Standards for English Language Arts and Literacy for Social Studies/ History, Science, and Technical Subjects define new expectations for instructional planning for many teachers. In particular, success with these new standards requires that students have regular and consistent practice reading, understanding, analyzing, and using complex texts. The time and purpose for the thoughtful teaching of these texts must be built into our unit plans.

It's important that all teachers learn to plan units this way, because meeting the challenge of teaching students with complex texts is essential. According to NAEP's most recent report, *Reading 2011*, less than half of fourth graders and fewer than forty percent of eighth graders are reading at a proficient level (2011). In a 2008 study, Gary Williamson, of the North Carolina Department of Public Instruction, found that high school students who could comfortably read and comprehend most typical high school texts may be able to access only the important ideas in "about one-fourth of the reading materials in military, citizenship, and workplace text collections and perhaps as little as five percent of postsecondary texts" (*A Text Readability Continuum for Postsecondary Readiness*, 2008). That's a lot of kids without the sophisticated tools they need for learning, and eventually, for working, surviving, and thriving. That's a lot of kids who need to be noticed.

Literacy is the gateway skill to success in the study of any content area, to success in any kind of postsecondary education, and to advanced training in trades and in the military. So the goal of the Common Core State Standards is right. But if we want the new standards to make a difference, we need to plan in ways that lead to change. Existing paradigms of planning, particularly paradigms that do not help students engage with and understand complex texts, will not be sufficient.

Achieving the goal of significantly improving students' capacity to read, think about, and comprehend complex texts will require teachers to take specific actions while planning. Those actions are briefly described below and are more fully articulated in each chapter of this book.

Commit to Articulating Long-Range Plans

Teaching is intense work. The work of the day rarely includes chunks of time adequate for the preparation of the actual teaching. In addition, spending the day being "on" for a group of kids is emotionally and intellectually draining. I can remember using my so-called planning periods merely to rest. Plus, there are always time-sensitive responsibilities that draw us away from planning—meetings, requests from students for help, phone calls, etc. There are plenty of reasons for teachers to be either replicating old unit plans in old patterns or planning day-to-day, just a lesson or two ahead of the kids in terms of where things are going, making tweaks as they go and throwing in reading where they think it might fit. But these new standards require an investment of time into the development of new, focused units that both students and teachers find interesting and worthwhile. The planning template and process described in Chapter 1 will help get you started thinking about the resources, time, and decisions needed to design new Common Core-aligned units.

Envision Contextualized Content

In many classrooms, particularly in those designed to help our most struggling readers, students are regularly engaged in decontextualized practice. They do not get deep into content, new ideas, or even texts, but instead skip from worksheet to worksheet, from drill to drill. Students like Josh need to be compelled by meaningful, appealing reasons to improve their literacy skills. This involves creating a context for learning that gives students a real-world purpose to read—especially to read complex text that requires extended focus and stamina. Context can come from in-depth investigations or projects, from purpose outside of the classroom, or from pairing or examining texts in unusual ways. The variety of options for contextualizing content described in Chapter 2 are designed to spark your thinking about how to make your students *want* to read.

Develop Student-Shared Goals

Adolescents seek to experiment with their emerging sense of autonomy, purpose, and power. Helping students understand the steps to learning and monitoring their own progress in meaningful ways results in increased engagement and improved learning. Once compelling curriculum has been conceived, teachers can work smarter by planning backwards to strategically develop and use carefully crafted, standards-based, student-friendly statements of intended learning—what Stiggins, Arter, Chappuis, and Chappuis (2012) call "learning targets"—to frame a longer-term chunk of learning, such as a unit or a project.

Learning targets are different from objectives; objectives are intended for teacher planning, and learning targets are intended for student use before, during, and after a learning episode. Learning targets help students understand what *learning* they are expected to do, as opposed to which activity they are expected to complete. Teachers who are committed to helping students meet the challenge of reading complex texts use learning targets to open conversations, not only about the content students are expected to master but also to demystify the reading process. Because of learning targets, Josh and I had a shared language to discuss what he needed to try to do differently. I used learning targets with kids to help them understand what actually happens in a proficient reader's mind, to help them understand specifically what they need to do to become better readers, and to help them track their progress toward meeting both content and literacy targets over time. Chapter 3 will help you develop and use learning targets well.

Select Strategies That Build Understanding

All too often, students are expected to think and "do" with text in the most surface of ways. With careful selection of critical-thinking strategies, teachers plan lessons in which the students are in charge of making the text make sense, as well as monitoring the students' progress.

We need to be very sure we are selecting strategies and texts that help our students develop the mental habits of great readers. Josh had come to believe that the purpose of reading was to find the answers to questions. His sole strategy was to keep re-reading until he found the answers he was looking for and to highlight them when he found them. Of course, that only worked some of the time, since many questions are answered in the mind, *based* on the text. No wonder Josh was defeated so often. Chapter 4 will help you find and implement the right strategies to help your students make meaning of complex texts.

Differentiate Purposefully

Differentiation is critical in terms of developing ALL students' capacity to read and understand complex text. But differentiation of literacy-based work must be used strategically and purposefully. When planning for differentiation in the general education classroom, teachers must focus on essential learning goals and maintain those goals for all students, even while offering variety and choice. Teachers must also maintain a clear and consistent vision of what students need to *become able to do* and always plan for continuous progress—not merely ask students to do what they already know how to do or are most comfortable with. Implementing the Common Core Standards means explicitly planning for student growth. Josh did not need me to differentiate the text he was reading, which was the most obvious choice. That kind of differentiation would have robbed him of access to the kind of text he most needed to learn to tackle. Most students need their tasks differentiated, not their texts, at least some of the time. Chapter 5 will help you differentiate well.

How to Read This "How To" Book

Start by reading Chapter 1 to discover the big ideas and central premise of this book—that planning is a long-term process that involves envisioning, careful crafting of learning targets, thoughtful selection of reading materials, the selection of strategies, differentiating, and reflecting on both the teaching and the learning. Then review the exemplar Common Core-aligned unit in Chapter 2 and think about the places where your own work is strong and where you need further development. The chapters that follow can be read in order, or you can pursue the chapters that most interest you or those that you think will most benefit your students. Each chapter contains specific examples, planning tools, and templates. I wish you the best on your journey of continuous improvement.

Works Cited

Guthrie, John T., and N. M. Humenick. 2004. "Motivating Students to Read: Evidence for Classroom Practices That Increase Reading Motivation and Achievement." In P. McCardle and V. Chhabra, eds., *The Voice of Evidence in Reading Research*, 329–354. Baltimore, MD: Paul Brookes Publishing.

Stiggins, Richard J., Judith A. Arter, Jan Chappuis, and Stephen Chappuis. 2012. *Classroom Assessment* for *Student Learning: Doing It Right—Using It Well*. Portland, OR: Assessment Training Institute, Inc.

Williamson, Gary L., 2008. "A Text Readability Continuum for Postsecondary Readiness." *Journal of Advanced Academics* 19: 602–632, doi:10.4219/jaa-2008-832.

CHAPTER ONE

ARTICULATE LONG-RANGE PLANS

Seeing the Need to Change

Paul Green and Michelle Park teach together as the eighth-grade humanities team in a middle school. For years, they collaborated on an integrated Holocaust unit. In Paul's class, the students analyzed the factors leading to the rise of Hitler and the worldwide impact of the Holocaust. In Michelle's class, the students read *The Diary of Anne Frank,* studied the poetry of Holocaust survivors, and wrote a research paper. The unit concluded with a visit from a Holocaust survivor, which brought the students up starkly against the reality of what they had studied.

This unit had always been a hit with the kids—the Holocaust is in and of itself compelling to students, and *The Diary of Anne Frank* resonates with them. Actually meeting with someone who had survived the Holocaust inevitably touched them deeply. After three years of teaching the unit together, Michelle and Paul felt very good about this segment of their school year. The kids were engaged, their partnership felt authentic and in sync, and frankly, they did not have to plan as much as they once did in order to make each day purposeful and productive.

As the Common Core Standards rolled out in their district, Michelle and Paul thought immediately of their Holocaust unit as an exemplar of expectations. Both teachers asked students to read during the unit, and the research paper definitely involved writing from primary sources. But as they studied the Introduction of the Common Core Standards and learned more about the levels of rigor needed to lift their middle schoolers' literacy skills, they began to rethink their definition of *exemplary*.

In the Introduction to the Common Core Standards is a "portrait of students who meet the standards" (2010, 7). This page describes a vision of students who are college and career ready, a vision that resonated with Michelle and Paul.

College- and career-ready students are:

> *Independent.* By the time they graduate from high school, they know how to read, question, learn from, and critique all kinds of complex texts.

> *Builders of content knowledge.* They can learn from reading and refine their learning through speaking and listening.

> *Flexible.* They can vary their speaking and writing to meet the needs of a variety of audiences, tasks, purposes, and disciplines. They can analyze situations and match their messages to their intentions and the needs of those around them.

> *Critical thinkers.* They can interpret, provide evidence for their thinking, and critique. They are aware of when others are attempting to influence them and can make reasoned, sound judgments.

> *Capable users of technological tools.* They use technology proficiently to enhance their understanding of information and to shape powerful messages.

> *Globally aware.* They know and respect perspectives and cultures beyond their own.

After reading this "portrait," Paul and Michelle realized that if they wanted to truly embrace the vision of college- and career-ready students, they had some changes to make, even to their best unit. It had the *potential* to be strongly aligned with the Common Core Standards if they thought more carefully about:

> ways to engage more students deeply in the process

> increasing the variety of texts that students read throughout the unit in both classrooms

> finding ways for students to think more critically about ideas and texts

> creating situations where the students' attention to tone and style really mattered to them.

Change at Both the Classroom and System Level

As Michelle, Paul, and I began to talk about revising their unit, I realized that while some of the decisions and changes they would make were entirely within their control, others were dependent on the larger system of their school and district. Seemingly simple things, like accessing new materials, were actually complex barriers to change. My work with this team prompted me to develop the following rubric to help teachers *and* leaders examine instructional plans for alignment to the Common Core Standards. I offered this rubric to the team not as a checklist but rather to provoke their thinking. I hoped it would help them open conversations, both between themselves and with their principal. If we are truly to create the kind of literate, critical thinkers as described in the "portrait of a student," what does it mean for the work of teachers, district and building leaders, the acquisition of resources, and the alignment of systems?

Note: A "unit" is a series of lessons, usually linked by a common concept, often resulting in a summative assessment.

Aligning Unit Plans with Common Core Literacy Standards

Major Shift	Emerging Alignment	Meaningful Alignment	Exemplary Alignment
Balancing Informational and Fictional Text (PreK–5)	Students read both fiction and nonfiction, mostly from basals and textbooks, throughout the day. Content-based units incorporate meaningful reading and writing tasks.	Students read a variety of trade books and textbooks, along with an assortment of literature, during reading lessons and content-focused lessons. Students are assigned related or paired fiction and nonfiction in the classroom, which they access in the library and on the Internet.	Students read not only textbooks and trade books during reading lessons and content-focused lessons, but also a variety of authentic, real-world texts. In addition to traditional school texts, students read scientific field guides, primary sources, artists' statements, and the like in order to explore big ideas and grapple with essential questions. Students are surrounded by the opportunity to learn from all kinds of texts.
Building Knowledge in the Disciplines (6–12)	Students read both fiction and nonfiction, mostly from textbooks, anthologies, and novels, throughout the day. Students read more nonfiction than fiction.	Students read a variety of trade books, nonfiction, and textbooks, along with an assortment of contemporary and classic literature, throughout the day. Students access both fiction and nonfiction in the classroom, the library, and on the Internet. The majority of students' reading is nonfiction.	Students read not only traditional school materials, but position papers, scientific journal articles, field guides, original research, primary sources, and the like to explore big ideas and grapple with essential questions. Students are surrounded by the opportunity to learn from and analyze the impact of all kinds of texts. Students are deeply engaged in reading worthy texts of all kinds.
Staircase of Complexity	Teachers determine the difficulty of text they plan to use and ensure that all students read grade-level texts at least some of the time. Students are supported through strategic instruction to actually read challenging texts.	Teachers determine the difficulty of texts they plan to use and purposefully increase the complexity of texts over the course of each unit/across the year. Students are supported to actually read challenging texts through strategic instruction planned following diagnostic assessment.	There's a school-wide system for determining complex core texts for each grade level and for ensuring that core texts become increasingly and appropriately rigorous over grade spans. Students are supported to actually read challenging texts through differentiated strategic instruction based on diagnostic assessment. Students show increasing independence with challenging texts.
Text-Based Answers	Students move away from simplistic connections, questions, and inferences and begin to justify responses, reactions, and understandings with evidence from the text.	Students justify their reactions and responses to text with evidence. Questions for discussion are carefully crafted to ensure that students must read closely for what the text does and does not say.	All of the previous criteria AND students engage in meaningful discussions and written analyses in which they support their opinions and ideas with evidence from the text.
Writing from Sources	Narrative writing is assigned less and is replaced with informational pieces and arguments, incorporating information from sources.	Students begin to expand on forms and develop a variety of informational and argumentative pieces. Writing is strengthened by information and evidence from a variety of sources.	Students read a variety of sources and write informational texts and arguments for authentic audiences or to serve a real need (e.g., to share the findings of original research or to convince a constituency to take action).
Academic Vocabulary	Students acquire academic vocabulary (e.g., Tier 2 words such as *consequently* or *intermittently*) through a wide range of reading and direct instruction, planned within the context of multiple units.	Students acquire academic vocabulary as a result of teachers' careful identification of important conceptual and "high power" Tier 2 words, within the context of multiple units. Vocabulary instruction goes beyond rote memorization.	Students acquire vocabulary through wide reading. Teachers use rich, research-based strategies to engage students in exploring, acquiring, and assimilating academic vocabulary into their speaking and writing on an ongoing basis.

Surface Change vs. Substantive Change

Right after analyzing the rubric, both Michelle and Paul made some changes at the lesson level by adding some challenging primary source documents into their lessons and by focusing more deliberately on teaching vocabulary. They also asked their principal to be sure that conversations about identifying and using appropriately complex texts, and taking a potentially more systematic approach to vocabulary instruction, were part of upcoming professional development offerings and faculty meeting conversations.

Then Michelle and Paul turned their attention to revising their unit more deeply. I asked them to start by showing me the planning documents they'd developed previously, and they realized that they had never fully articulated their unit plans. They didn't have long-term objectives written anywhere. Paul had never actually outlined any specific plans to teach students how to read or analyze primary source documents. Michelle had never discerned which specific standards she was assessing in any given ELA unit. Essentially, they had their Holocaust unit stored in several binders of resources, and there was ongoing discontent with the rubric for their research paper.

Paul, Michelle, and I spent several days together that summer re-envisioning their Holocaust unit. Both came to the task with new ideas and had spent time researching and reading new material prior to our working together. After lots of messy brainstorming, more reading, discussing, and throwing ideas out of the window, we recast the purpose of the unit to be not simply a study of the Holocaust, but a story of bullies, bystanders, and heroes. We carefully articulated the Standards that would be deliberately taught and assessed in the unit. We shifted the research paper from a separate, lengthy process to an embedded process, resulting in cited notes and a public service announcement. And we wrote everything down.

"The more time I spend getting really clear on the big picture, the more my lessons make sense," Michelle reflected as we completed this summer work. "It is hard to commit to the large blocks of planning time it takes to do this. They aren't really built into our schedule. We just have to be strategic about summer work, or pick a date to stay late, or do a Saturday and gut it out. It's worth it. If I don't do it, my lessons become just a series of activities rather than a deliberate scaffolding of learning. I think of the time spent articulating clearer plans as an investment, personally, because although it's hard to commit the time, I always feel more in control after I've done it."

Paul and Michelle completed the following unit planning template to formalize their thinking about their now more Common Core-aligned unit.

UNIT NAME:

Bullies, Bystanders, and Heroes: The Holocaust Grade 8

Overview

In this unit, students read, write, listen, and speak to understand the power struggles that led to World War II, the devastation of the War, and the Holocaust in particular. Students will carefully and closely read a variety of primary and secondary sources, with an emphasis on selecting evidence to support their thinking, answering strategic questions, and comparing multiple versions of various events. Students will write essays in both Social Studies and ELA, but their ultimate performance task will involve providing a public service announcement that incorporates a claim and evidence.

Context

Students will study the Holocaust through the lens of the bully cycle. They will learn how bullies use their power to intimidate and disempower others, thus creating bystanders, and the steps that heroes take in order to protect victims from bullies. Although the events and forces leading up to the Holocaust are more complex than the dynamics of bullying, this context gives students a perspective on people's fear of standing up to Hitler and his regime and an appreciation for the necessity of overcoming similar fears in their own lives.

Guiding Questions

What factors and forces allow a minority to control, and even destroy, a majority?

What choices must people face when confronted with injustice?

Why do some people stand by while others stand up?

Standards/Key Ideas Assessed in This Unit: Social Studies

Grade 8 Social Studies

Use a variety of intellectual skills to demonstrate an understanding of major ideas, eras, themes, developments, and turning points in world history and examine the broad sweep of history from a variety of perspectives. (New York State Learning Standards for Social Studies 1996)

Grade 8 Literacy in History/Social Studies

RH.6-8.1 Cite specific textual evidence to support analysis of primary and secondary sources.

RH.6-8.2 Determine the central ideas or information of a primary or secondary source; provide an accurate summary of the source distinct from prior knowledge or opinions.

RH.6-8.6 Identify aspects of a text that reveal an author's point of view or purpose (e.g., loaded language, inclusion or avoidance of particular facts).

WHST.6-8.1 Write arguments focused on *discipline-specific content.*

Long-Term Targets	Supporting Targets	Assessments
I can describe the nature of warfare during World War II.	I can identify key causes of World War II. I can summarize key documents to analyze the aggressive powers of Japan, Italy, and Germany. I can explain the United States' initial desire to remain neutral. I can describe wartime strategies, such as collaboration and resistance.	Quizzes Unit test Primary source document analysis worksheets and summaries (Shared with ELA) Claim-Evidence-Interpretation notes
I can describe the consequences, including the human atrocities, of World War II.	Through close reading of primary and secondary sources, I can analyze the origins of the Holocaust. Through close reading of primary and secondary sources, I can trace the course of the Holocaust.	Summary Wheel Reading from Different Perspectives organizers Unit test
I can analyze the need for the United Nations.	I can trace the origin of and initial impact of the United Nations.	United Nations document-based scaffolding questions and essay

Standards/Key Ideas Assessed in This Unit: English Language Arts

RL. and RI.8.1 Cite the textual evidence that most strongly supports an analysis of what the text says explicitly as well as inferences drawn from the text.

RL. and RI.8.2 Determine a theme or central idea of a text and analyze its development over the course of the text, including its relationship to the characters, setting, and plot; provide an objective summary of the text.

RL.8.3 Analyze how particular lines of dialogue or incidents in a story or drama propel the action, reveal aspects of a character, or provoke a decision.

RL.8.6 Analyze how differences in the points of view of the characters and the audience or reader (e.g., created through the use of dramatic irony) create such effects as suspense or humor.

RI.8.9 Analyze a case in which two or more texts provide conflicting information on the same topic and identify where the texts disagree on matters of fact or interpretation.

W.8.1 Write arguments to support claims with clear reasons and relevant evidence.

W.8.2 Write informative/explanatory texts to examine a topic and convey ideas, concepts, and information through the selection, organization, and analysis of relevant content.

W.8.5 With some guidance and support from peers and adults, develop and strengthen writing as needed by planning, revising, editing, rewriting, or trying a new approach, focusing on how well purpose and audience have been addressed.

Long-Term Targets	Supporting Targets	Assessments
I can cite evidence from a variety of texts to compare the roles and typical incidents embedded in the "bully cycle" to the events leading to and including the Holocaust.	I can read closely to select evidence relevant to my purpose. I can form a claim and support it with evidence from texts.	Analysis and observation of students' annotations Answers to strategic questions (Shared with Social Studies) Claim-Evidence-Interpretation notes
I can analyze plot, characterization, and the development of theme in *The Diary of Anne Frank* and related literature.	I can determine how dialogue and incidents propel the story of the Frank family. I can analyze how particular scenes and incidents impact me as a reader. I can determine and reflect on the themes in *The Diary of Anne Frank* and related literature.	Answers to strategic questions It Says/I Say/And So response notes Collaborative Comprehension discussion notes and observations Theme quickwrite

continues

Long-Term Targets	Supporting Targets	Assessments
I can compare and contrast texts and firsthand accounts that describe the same events in different ways.	I can determine how Anne and Miep's differing perspectives shape their thinking and actions. I can determine how speeches by Morgan and Niemöller are similar and different. I can compare and contrast the experiences of an actual Holocaust survivor with what I have learned from reading. I can introduce my topic clearly, previewing what is to follow. I can develop my essay with relevant, concrete details and quotations, and other examples that are organized to support my reader. I can use appropriate and varied transitions to create cohesion and clarify the relationships among ideas and concepts. I can use precise language and domain-specific vocabulary to inform about or explain the topic. I can provide a concluding statement or section that follows from and supports the information or explanation presented.	Double Entry Journals Compare and Contrast organizers Explanatory essay
I can use the writing process to create a compelling anti-bullying argument, drawing on a variety of sources to prove my claim.	I can analyze speeches by Morgan and Niemöller as models of argument. I can introduce claim(s) and acknowledge and distinguish the claim(s) from alternate or opposing claims. I can support claim(s) with logical reasoning and relevant evidence, using accurate, credible sources and demonstrating an understanding of the topic or text. I can organize reasons and evidence logically. I can use words, phrases, and clauses to create a logical flow that my reader can follow. I can establish and maintain a style that enhances my message. I can conclude my piece in a way that follows from and supports the argument presented. I can improve my work through feedback and revision.	Reflection on Holocaust survivor feedback Public service announcement scripts

Product Descriptor

Students will produce a public service announcement integrating a claim and evidence, designed to influence teens to become a "hero" rather than a "bystander" when observing or becoming otherwise aware of bullying situations. Students will write and revise a script showing the integration of details, facts, images, and other information that they have read over the course of the unit in both primary and secondary sources. Students will also create a technically accurate bibliography. Once students have at least met these standards for the script and bibliography, they will then use iMovie to create their PSAs.

Script Rubric

	Exceeds Standard	Meets Standards	Approaching Standards	Far from Standards
Claim	Claim shows deep, insightful comprehension of the issue. Claim is powerful and captures the attention of the audience.	Claim shows fundamental comprehension of the issue. Claim is straightforward and clear.	Claim shows surface level or confused comprehension of the issue. Claim is present but not stirring or clear.	Claim shows lack of comprehension of the issue. Claim is absent.
Evidence	Evidence is thorough and convincing and selected from a broad variety of sources.	Reasonable evidence is selected from several sources.	Evidence is underdeveloped or selected from only one source.	A lack of evidence weakens the impact of the piece.
Organization	Claim and evidence are seamlessly integrated into a powerful, logical argument. Skillful and varied transitions guide the audience to the point.	Evidence follows the claim in a logical pattern. The author uses transitions to connect ideas.	Evidence follows the claim in a haphazard order. Some transitions are used to connect ideas.	It is difficult to discern an organizational pattern to the piece. The lack of transitions makes it challenging for the audience to follow the piece.
Style	Tone is convincing and mature. Precise words are chosen for maximum effect on the audience.	Tone is generally convincing. The author uses vocabulary appropriate to the task.	Tone is striving to be convincing but is inconsistent. The author sometimes falls back on simplistic vocabulary.	The tone is ineffective for the task. The author often falls back on simplistic vocabulary.
Conventions	The work is technically precise. An error may exist, but it is in an area in which the author is taking risks with new words or techniques.	The work contains a few noticeable errors, but they do not interfere with the audience's comprehension.	The work contains many noticeable errors, enough to be distracting to the audience.	The work contains many errors that interfere with the audience's understanding of the message.

Expected Complexity Band for Grade 8: 925–1185 Lexile		
Core Texts	**Quantitative Complexity**	**Qualitative Complexity**
"Understanding Bullying Fact Sheet," Centers for Disease Control and Prevention	Lexile—1270	Written for adults. Medical/technical vocabulary. Well organized with subheadings.
Video: "A Time to Speak," a speech by Charles Morgan	N/A	Challenging content, including racial slurs.
"Kids Are Worth It," Bully Handout for Teens	N/A—graphic	Accessible, but we must tend to layout on the page; not fully intuitive.
"First They Came for the Communists," a speech by Martin Niemöller	Lexile—890	Requires inference re: "communists" and "trade unions" in order to fully comprehend.
The Diary of a Young Girl, Anne Frank and Otto Frank	Lexile—1080	Readers are supported by familiar diary style. Straightforward narrative structure. Advanced, unfamiliar vocabulary.
Excerpts from *Schindler's List* by Thomas Keneally	Lexile—1150	Many readers are familiar with the story, so it's OK to take some excerpts out of context.
Excerpts from *Anne Frank Remembered: The Story of the Woman Who Helped to Hide the Frank Family*, Meip Gies and Allison Leslie Gold	Lexile—920	Clear narrative throughline. Some advanced vocabulary.
Primary source documents: Hate propaganda	Various	Disturbing content. High levels of inferential thinking required.
Primary source documents: The Jewish Foundation for the Righteous	Various	Disturbing content. High levels of inferential thinking required.

The Steps in Long-Range Planning

In completing the unit plan overview, Michelle and Paul had begun the process of planning to align to the Common Core Standards. This articulated, long-range planning—up front—is the first step in a long-term process that includes envisioning a unit, delivering it while monitoring and adjusting, and reflecting on it both to revise for the next year and to inform your next teaching steps.

Planning includes everything teachers do in order to use the approximately thirty hours a week they *do* spend with students in ways that result in maximized learning. This includes: examining and analyzing standards and curriculum documents, mapping out the big chunks of a year's worth of instruction, determining unit- and lesson-level objectives, designing or selecting assessments, collecting or creating resources, and crafting activities through which students will engage in work and thinking. In addition, effective planning includes a written or mental rehearsal of the way a particular instructional period will unfold. This necessitates careful thinking about the sequence of events, possible questions to ask, the movement of students and materials, and potential pitfalls. Planning is multifaceted and time consuming, but doing it well is essential in order to realize the full potential of the goals and purposes of the Common Core Standards.

High-quality planning also involves deeply and carefully documenting teachers' thinking. I am amazed by how much curriculum lives merely in teachers' heads. There are three things wrong with this. First, writing is a form of thinking and clarifying. Articulating plans through writing forces teachers to think deeply about their choices and cross-check that they are making the right choices. Second, writing is a form of decision making, and writing things down helps teachers commit to intentional teaching, resulting in less drift from intended outcomes. Finally, writing curriculum creates the possibility of ongoing feedback, and feedback helps strengthen plans. As I worked with Michelle and Paul over the course of several months to plan and bring their Holocaust unit into tighter alignment with the Common Core Standards, we moved through the following stages together, documenting as we went.

Up Front: Envisioning an Immediately Relevant Context and Product

Michelle and Paul's original Holocaust unit had been engaging to most students merely because of its subject matter. However, their shift to include a great deal more complex text in the unit, as required by the Common Core Standards, led them to worry about engaging their students who were most challenged by reading. They needed to create a "hook" that would instill in all readers a desire to dig into the challenge of complex text, thus came about the idea of comparing the roles and actions of bullies, bystanders, and heroes to the roles, people, and events of the Holocaust. The teachers decided that students should deeply understand the conditions that led to Hitler's rise and his capacity to influence people as parallel to a bully's capacity to create fear and silence within the bystanders. In this way, the Holocaust could be more than a historical event; it could also be a cautionary tale regarding the kind of behavior many middle schoolers engage in and experience every day. We eventually captured all of this thinking—all parts of the "envisioning" stage of planning—in the unit template. This concept of contextualizing content, or wrapping it in relevant meaning for students, is explored more deeply in Chapter 2.

Stages in Long-Range Planning for Implementing the Common Core Reading Standards

	Timing	Stage	Purpose	Documents Created
Up Front	Well in advance of teaching the unit	Envisioning	Creating a compelling purpose or context that engages students in developing and practicing their literacy skills. This often takes reading and research on the part of the teachers and most likely happens sporadically throughout a teacher's career.	Descriptive Overview portion of the unit plan Context and Guiding Questions portions of the unit plan
		Planning product, performance, or assessment	Beginning to align work to Standards and determine a rigorous end goal for the unit that engages students in reading, writing, listening, and/or speaking.	Standards-Targets-Assessment portion of the unit plan Product or Performance descriptor or actual assessment, along with criteria for success and a rubric
		Selecting	Choosing reading materials at the right levels of complexity, as well as supplemental materials for differentiation.	Core texts list portion of unit plan, including quantitative and qualitative measures of complexity
	Approaching the teaching of the unit	Strategizing	Determining the needs of the actual students to be taught. Might suggest the addition or subtraction of certain Standards or texts, as well as inform the pedagogical choices.	Pre-assessment Matrix (see Chapter 5)
			Developing, perhaps with colleagues, the teacher moves that will help all students deeply engage in "just right" work. Calendaring the intended lessons.	Calendar that articulates daily targets, strategies, and formative assessments
Implementing	As the unit unfolds	Monitoring	Adjusting the timeline and lessons based on what learners are coming to know and be able to do and what they need to know more of and do more of. Locating and creating the day-to-day lessons and materials. Using assessment for learning strategies and micro-adjusting for individual students and small groups of students. Using information to develop new understanding of trends and patterns for the next unit.	Adjusted Calendar Lesson plans (including Close-Reading lesson plan, see page 67)
Reflecting	After the unit	Reflecting	Looking back to determine what worked best and what should be adjusted for the next time. Take a close look at "target" students, as predictors of trends.	Revisions to unit plans—both the one just finished and the one coming up next

Another way Michelle and Paul decided to hook their students into deeper reading was to revise the final product for the unit from a research paper to a well-researched public service announcement, in which students would combine primary sources from the Holocaust along with carefully crafted messages about bullying so that other teens might choose to be heroes rather than bystanders. The teachers saw a real need for this product and thought that their students would too. In addition, they thought students' clarity about the audience they would be communicating with would motivate the students to complete high-quality work worthy of a life beyond the classroom.

Toward that end, instead of asking a single Holocaust survivor to visit the class at the end of the unit, the teachers decided to ask a group of Holocaust survivors to visit several times—once to tell their stories, again to provide feedback on the public service announcement drafts, and finally to a "showing" of the final PSAs. The teachers thought this kind of real-world interaction and feedback would also impact the students' desire to persist with challenging work.

Michelle and Paul's commitment to planning an authentic final product for their unit—and planning it early in the game (notice it's the second thing on the chart)—was a critical move in terms of amping up the rigor and Common Core-alignment of their unit. In the past, students' research papers about various aspects of the Holocaust had always felt like an add-on, because in fact, they were. The research did not serve any specific purpose, and the students completed it after they had already learned a great deal about the Holocaust. The early work of the unit did not lead to the research paper because the two were only loosely linked.

By planning the PSA as their second step rather than their last step, Michelle and Paul could then progress more thoughtfully into planning the lessons, resources, and experiences their students would need from the beginning of the unit in order to successfully reach the end. This process, called "backward design" by Grant Wiggins and Jay McTighe in their seminal book *Understanding by Design* (2005), seems commonly known although sometimes still not practiced. Knowing where you're going is an essential step toward getting there.

Up Front: Selecting a Variety of Resources to Meet All Students' Needs

With the end in mind, Michelle and Paul moved into the selecting phase of up-front unit planning. They decided to keep *The Diary of Anne Frank* as the anchor text for the unit, since it features Frank family protector Miep Gies in the role of the hero, but they added a varied selection of complex and less complex primary source documents, including excerpts from Gies' own book, along with a variety of reading and viewing materials from anti-bullying campaigns, both modern and historical.

Paul, Michelle, and I read the texts together to plan close-reading lessons framed by strategic, text-dependent lessons. We highlighted the academic vocabulary in the texts for the students to learn and discuss in context, particularly for when strategic questions were used to shine a light on those important new words. This work of really digging into the texts themselves made ongoing lesson planning, once the unit was in play, more focused and purposeful. There's more advice about selecting appropriate texts in Chapter 2.

Up Front: Strategizing to Match the Plans to Actual Kids

About two months before the teachers intended to deliver their new unit, I met with them and the team's special education teacher, along with an ELL specialist, to consider our plans in light of the needs of their students. Collectively, the group agreed that using the "bully, bystander, and hero" materials as the "hook" into the unit would be engaging for all students and would help them build background, which would help them make connections when the Holocaust content was studied.

The team decided to develop a case study of a bullying situation that students would study deeply in order to develop generalizations about bullying dynamics. This would serve as a lens for their Holocaust study. Since most of the bullying materials Michelle and Paul had found the summer before were written for young teens, and because many of them were video-based, the team felt that this was an accessible entry point to the unit for all students. Michelle and Paul both agreed to spend time on the case study at the beginning of the unit so that kids would see their partnership and the connection between the two classrooms. Michelle shared which portions of *The Diary of Anne Frank* she intended to use as close-reading exercises, and she demonstrated a new strategy for text annotating that the group agreed was worth a try and that the special education and ELL teacher both agreed to reinforce.

In addition, the teachers determined that a jigsaw approach to the study of several of the primary source documents would enable all students to work with documents that were at "just right" reading levels for them. The teachers sorted all of the documents and pre-labeled the ones that would be best for specific students. Then they laid out a calendar for the development of the public service announcements that they intended to distribute to the students to help them stay on track. Next, they decided which students would get more support during the research phase of the PSA development by having specific websites marked for them and by using a highly structured note-taking process. In addition, the group decided that this smaller group of students would have their progress checked more often. The special education teacher made a modified planning calendar for this smaller group of students, which reflected their differentiated process. Finally, the teachers recognized that the special education and ELL students would benefit from supplemental direct instruction in the vocabulary that had been chosen by Michelle and Paul. Chapter 4 will help you build your strategy toolkit. For more support with purposeful differentiation, see Chapter 5.

Implementing: Monitoring Along the Way

I checked in with the team when they first started the unit and again, midway. Paul and Michelle both agreed that starting the unit with the bullying case study gave it new life and also revealed a clump of kids who struggled with reading grade-level text. They were planning to adjust their primary source study to ensure that these students had access to primary sources they could work with, and Michelle would keep a close eye on these students during the close-reading exercises, pushing them to participate fully. Both teachers agreed that some of these same students who were struggling would benefit from the modified planning calendar for the PSA. In addition, they felt their hook had particularly engaged two boys who hadn't shown much motivation for reading and writing so far that year. Midway through the unit, the teachers were psyched about the connection students were making between the bullies and bystanders hook and the Holocaust. Paul felt the kids had a deeper understanding about why the repressed German people "went along" with Hitler, and Michelle was excited about the enthusiasm the students were showing for their PSA project. The feedback being provided by the Holocaust survivors was impacting the students; they wanted to get their final products right.

I was present the night the final PSAs were shown, and the students' work blew me away. Their PSAs were carefully crafted—every word mattered—and the precision and evidence built into their messages suggested they had learned a great deal. Their parents, and the Holocaust survivors who came for the showing, were deeply touched. The principal decided to share the audio from the PSAs during morning announcements, and several of the PSAs were linked to the district's website to show the quality of work that engaged, motivated middle school students could create.

The Final Stage: Reflecting

We met one last time to celebrate the work that Michelle and Paul had put into their revised unit and the impact that their decisions had made on their students. As we reflected on their Bullies, Bystanders, and Heroes unit, Michelle and Paul talked specifically about three students who, for them, represented "types" of students that they often worried about. Daquan was one of their most capable readers and writers. He studied several very challenging primary source documents, including selections from *Mein Kampf* that he found online, and brought what he learned from those texts into the study of Anne Frank's diary, often making inferences that deepened the whole class' understanding. He took his study of the bullies and bystanders cycle beyond the classroom, and his PSA was powerful.

Victor was often less engaged than his teachers hoped he would be, but this particular unit seemed to light a fire in him. He actively sought feedback on his PSA and revised it several times, weaving in new information from independent research.

Christine was a struggling reader who predictably struggled to read all of the text in the unit that was above her fifth-grade reading level. However, both teachers felt she was very successful during the primary source study when texts were differentiated for her, and that this success, plus a solid structure for close reading and strategic questioning, gave her the boost she needed to persist when reading was more difficult. Michelle noted that Christine attempted to use context clues when the text was challenging and that she used five of the unit's vocabulary words in her PSA.

Michelle and Paul both remarked that the time they spent on the "big picture" of their unit—the envisioning, product planning, and selecting phases—made the other phases not only possible but also excellent. Without their attention to creating a compelling context for their unit and to finding a variety of resources, the differentiation that followed would have been fuzzy. Students would have learned *something*, for sure, but Michelle and Paul felt as if their students learned the *right stuff*, and *more of it*, and that they taught more intentionally, because of their long-term, articulated planning process.

Keys to Help You Make This Critical Move

> Planning to meet the expectations of the Common Core Standards involves deep change in instruction, resources, and systems.

> Articulating long-range plans in writing increases alignment and intentionality.

> Planning involves an investment of time up front to envision a context, plan an aligned product or performance, and select materials and strategies.

> Planning also involves ongoing monitoring and reflection.

Works Cited

Clark, Christopher M., and Robert J. Yinger. 1980. "The Hidden World of Teaching: Implications of Research on Teacher Planning." *Research Series No. 77* East Lansing, MI: Institute for Research on Teaching.

Wiggins, Grant, and Jay McTighe. 2005. *Understanding by Design.* Alexandria, VA: Association for Supervision & Curriculum Development.

CHAPTER TWO

ENVISION CONTEXTUALIZED CONTENT

How Will Andrew Respond?

When I first started teaching high school English, I defined my units by the list of books approved by my school district and the papers and projects I asked students to complete in connection with or in response to those books. I had a *Scarlet Letter* unit and a research paper unit, for example. The notion that books were my content was reinforced by the "curriculum" that was provided to me—a list of book titles and the requirement that students read four books from column A and at least one book from columns B and C, as well as write a certain number of papers. Even as I learned more about unit planning and sharpened my practice through concepts such as backward design, I still believed that my primary planning goal was to devise a series of lessons based on the content of novels and the development of several substantial papers.

Not too long into teaching, however, I came to realize that I also had to carefully consider my students' skill development in my planning. I began to weave strategy instruction into my units, helping students to think about how their brains worked when they were reading and writing. I planned minilessons and think-alouds to help my students understand more about the process of reading and writing. I thought I was doing pretty well with unit planning once I began to balance the dual pressures of ensuring that my students knew both *about* great books and *how to approach* books in general.

Then I met Andrew, an aloof ninth grader who pushed me every day with his sarcastic cracks about the complete lack of value he was finding in school in general, and in my class in particular. Andrew was whip-smart but simply didn't care to work hard on school assignments, particularly if they were challenging to him. In his mind (and likely in the minds of many of his classmates who just weren't bold enough to say so), reading novels for the sake of knowing what they were about and how to read them well was the biggest waste of time he could imagine.

Andrew's attitude haunted my planning sessions. I found myself internally judging my plans by whether or not he was going to respond favorably to what I had in mind. That favorable return was rare, but eventually I noticed a pattern. Andrew engaged when there was a purpose to a text or a task beyond its academic value.

I finally hit a sweet spot with Andrew when I stepped back from my district's list of books and began to question *why* I was teaching them. Although I loved and appreciated those novels, it was dawning on me that a needed to package them in ways that appealed to my students. I began envisioning these "packages," what I have come to call *contexts*.

Walking a Mile in Boo Radley's Shoes

It was during this time that I hatched an idea to wrap the novel *To Kill a Mockingbird* in a broader context. I'd always liked the novel's message of never really knowing another person until you walk a mile in his or her shoes. Hoping to help my students feel, rather than just read about, empathy, I kicked off the unit and their reading of *To Kill a Mockingbird* by announcing that we were organizing a shoe and boot drive, with the intention of donating warm footwear to a local homeless shelter prior to the arrival of that winter's snow. As we read the novel, a pile of shoes and boots grew in the corner of the classroom. Students made connections between Boo Radley's "invisibility" and the often unseen lives of the homeless. We mentally tried to "walk a mile" by researching about homelessness and writing stories about homeless people's lives from the perspective of the shoes on their feet. We wrote letters asking for donations. We wrote to the principal, asking for permission for a small group of us to go to the shelter to drop of the donations, and we wrote to the manager of the shelter, letting him know what we were up to.

From the minute I announced the shoe and boot drive, Andrew was fired up. He started reading—not just *To Kill a Mockingbird*—but everything he could find about homelessness. He brought in more shoes and boots than any other member of the class, thus earning his spot on the team that was going to the shelter. When we were at the shelter, he helped to clean and organize supplies. Andrew bought a brown corduroy suit from the shelter's resale shop and wore it proudly to the Sadie Hawkins dance. He changed from a mouthy, frustrating nonreader into a committed young adult, proud of his effort to reach out to others.

I learned a very important lesson from Andrew about planning smarter. I already knew that planning a unit with a text at its core is hard work. For starters, you have to read carefully yourself and develop a deep understanding of the text you want, or are required, to teach. You have to think about your students and the skills they need to develop. You have to think about pacing—how much can kids do with a text? How many days will it take for the students to do their work well? You have to think about structures, such as journals and discussion protocols and formative and summative assessments. You have to design lessons that are aligned with writing tasks. You have to find or prepare the materials you will need for every single day of instruction.

If your curriculum intersects in any way with others', such as special educators or intervention specialists, you have to involve them in all of these decisions. But what I learned from Andrew is that I needed to determine the "why" for every unit I developed. *Why* should students read any given text or texts? *Why* should they dig in and read texts closely? *Why* should they progress from the beginning to the end of a unit, likely encountering difficulties and frustrations along the way? Planning to meet the challenge of teaching complex texts begins with establishing a compelling "why" that drives students to read, think, write, talk, and sometimes act.

Planning a Compelling Context for Reading

The notion of planning compelling contexts for reading—what Andrew was crying out for—is affirmed by the research of Michael Smith and Jeffrey Wilhelm, as discussed in their book *Reading Don't Fix No Chevys: Literacy in the Lives of Young Men* (2002). The book delves into the issues that surround boys and literacy through interviews with forty-nine young men, an examination of their reading logs, and the use of think-aloud protocols by the boys when they read. Smith and Wilhelm's research showed that boys (and many girls) who call themselves "nonreaders" and who don't participate much in school-assigned reading, actually read outside of school to solve problems and learn things they want to know. In fact, the students in the study often said they were willing to read difficult material when it helped them learn something they considered important. Ultimately, these authors conclude that asking boys (and many girls) to read for the sake of reading is at the heart of students' disengagement from school-assigned reading. Smith and Wilhelm recommend that teachers make school literacy more compelling by creating contexts in which students feel the need to read.

Fortunately, there isn't just one "right" way to develop compelling contexts for reading. This is one really important area in the art of teaching where teachers can—with precise planning—use their creativity to bring their teaching alive. I sometimes use the metaphor of vanilla cake to explain the idea of creating contextualized curriculum. The Standards, and the materials that represent them, are vanilla cake. They are pretty good, but they are generic and plain. Some kids eat the plain cake but lots of kids don't. Context is delicious frosting. It's what you wrap the cake in to make it spectacular. Students who eventually "eat" the contextualized curriculum—the frosted cake—ingest all of the Standards that are baked into the cake plus the frosting, which makes the cake worth eating. It's the frosting that's spread all over the top, sides, and between the layers of the cake that draws students into the act of eating it. And teachers get to decide what flavor of frosting to use.

There are many ways to frost the Standards cake, and some of them might already be familiar to you. Students can read complex texts, write from sources, and listen and speak in order to:

> grapple with an intriguing question or test an interesting theory

> investigate a local injustice, problem, or concern

> teach others about compelling local history

> examine events or ideas from multiple perspectives

> analyze texts for what they have to teach about authorship and craft.

No matter what flavor (or flavors) of frosting you choose, there's one guiding principle I want you to remember as you read through the next several pages. All of these approaches are more rigorous if they are applied in ways that engage readers across *multiple texts*. Planning Common Core-aligned contexts for reading should consistently require readers to think critically, both *within* challenging texts and *across* challenging texts. As you design and plan new Common Core-aligned units, you should be thinking about "sets of texts," rather than "a text." Ideally, these sets of texts are richly varied and represent a balance of fiction and nonfiction—novels, literary nonfiction, poems, essays, speeches, primary sources, short stories, newspaper and magazine articles, websites, plays, textbooks, scientific papers, brochures, pamphlets, government reports—all of these things are fair game for a text set. If, after you've planned, you could still name your unit "*Name of Book with a Short Story and an Article Added*," you'll know you're not quite there yet.

Using Intriguing Questions to Test Theories

One way to plan smart, Common Core-aligned curriculum is by grouping texts to provide students with the opportunity to grapple with a compelling question or to test an intriguing theory. Many teachers are familiar with Wiggins and McTighe's concept of an "essential question," but from what I observe of teachers using this approach, there's a lot of confusion out there about what actually constitutes an essential question.

Wiggins and McTighe define essential questions as "questions that are not answerable with finality in a brief sentence. . . . Their aim is to stimulate thought, to provoke inquiry, and to spark more questions—including thoughtful student questions—not just pat answers" (106). This means that they are inherently more complex than what I usually observe and have come to call "focus questions." Focus questions are the day-by-day objective-based questions that students can answer within the course of a class or a couple of class periods, such as "What series of events lead to the deaths of Romeo and Juliet?" or "Was what Young Goodman Brown saw in the woods real or imagined?" Notice how both of those focus questions could be answered from just one text. Although essential questions *could* be written based on just one text, I find that there's a deep relationship between grouping texts for long-term study and excellent essential questions. A litmus test for knowing if you have really designed an essential question is that students will need multiple complex texts to really dig into it.

Wiggins and McTighe teach that essential questions refer to the "core ideas and inquiries within a discipline" (108). So it makes sense, then, that teachers might begin to write essential questions by studying the Common Core ELA Standards. For example:

Common Core Anchor Standards for Reading	Possible Essential Questions
Analyze how and why individuals, events, or ideas develop and interact over the course of a text.	Why do characters change? In what order is a story best told?
Assess how point of view or purpose shapes the content and style of a text.	Do narrators always tell the truth?
Common Core Anchor Standards for Writing	
Write arguments to support claims in an analysis of substantive topics or texts using valid reasoning and relevant and sufficient evidence.	How do you win an argument?

Questions like these become rich and intriguing when teachers deliberately group texts to make formulating and supporting an answer difficult. For example, "Do narrators always tell the truth?" becomes rich when students read short stories, poems, and speeches along a continuum from dispassionate to persuasive.

The questions in the chart above are solid, and they do represent the core ideas of the English Language Arts, but I (and, I believe, my students) have always been drawn more to the kinds of questions that encompass the ideas being studied in addition to the literary skills being developed. So, when writing essential questions, I am more likely to develop those like the following:

Text Sets	Possible Essential Questions
"Man vs. Wild" Nathaniel Hawthorne's *Young Goodman Brown*; Jon Krakauer's *Into the Wild*; Theodore Roosevelt's remarks upon the establishment of America's National Parks; Margaret Murie's essay *Two at Lobo Lake*	Why do narrators leave some things unsaid? AND Should mankind tame the wilderness?
"The Perfect Storm" Primary source documents related to the Dust Bowl; Timothy Egan's *The Worst Hard Time*; scientific reports related to the Dust Bowl; *China's Dust Storms Raise Fears of Impending Catastrophe*, National Geographic online	How important are the details? AND Who rules: mankind or Mother Nature?
"Invisible Men" Selections from Ralph Ellison's *The Invisible Man*; Edwin Arlington Robinson's poem "Richard Cory," *To Kill a Mockingbird* by Harper Lee	Why disconnect the mood from the meaning? AND What does it mean to be "seen"?

Freya Mercer is a middle school English Language Arts teacher in a small, rural school district in central New York who has found success in hooking her students by developing units that push them to test supposed "truths." One example from Freya's classroom comes from the way she introduces students to Shakespeare. "You've all heard of Shakespeare, right?" she asks. Her kids have; they know he's a famous author of plays. Some even know that he wrote in "old England." They know that his plays involve "not normal talking." And they are certain, absolutely certain, that he wrote *Romeo and Juliet* and some other famous poetry stuff. Then Freya throws them for a loop. "What would you say if I told you some scholars believe that Shakespeare *didn't* write these plays and sonnets?" she says. The students are outraged. It's like telling five-year-olds there's no Santa Claus.

Freya then uses two essential questions to launch her students into a short research project designed to help them decide, and defend their decisions, as to whether or not the plays and sonnets "by" William Shakespeare were really written by him. "Who really owns a story?" she asks them. "Can imagination overcome education?" Her students, by now anxious to determine whether they've been fed a bill of goods about this character Shakespeare, receive folders of articles that take both sides. They work within small groups to read all of the articles, develop a claim about whether or not Shakespeare should be credited with the work he is credited with, and gather details to support their claims and refute counterclaims. Freya selects the articles deliberately; she doesn't want this to be an easy decision for her students to make or defend. She wants students to have to really think while they are reading and re-reading. She wants them to decide about something that's not black and white, and then have to go back to the text to select the right details. When students have determined their positions, Freya engages them in a Socratic Seminar (a text-based, student-led discussion) around the essential questions, pushing them back to the texts they've read to make inferences about why there would be a mystery about this topic at all. The students don't complain about all of the reading they are doing. In fact, they hardly seem to notice that they are doing all of this reading work. Solving the "problem" of Shakespearean authorship motivates the students to read and think.

Designing units contextualized by questions and theories is a recursive, chicken-and-egg process. Sometimes, you have a great question or stumble across a mystery that kids will find compelling. In that case, the next step is to search out the texts that will bring the question or mystery into focus. Other times, perhaps more often because many schools and districts have defined sets of books that must be taught, you must sit back and consider the heart of the texts you are expected to teach. Ask yourself and your colleagues the following questions:

> › Why teach this text?
>
> › What questions does it raise about life, humanity, and the interconnectedness or disconnectedness between self and others?
>
> › How can I narrow or distill that set of questions into something compelling to the students I teach?
>
> › What does this text particularly show readers about the author's craft?
>
> › What could this text show my students about their own work as readers?
>
> › What other texts raise the same questions and offer other answers?
>
> › What would be revealed if I connected this text to others like it?
>
> › What would be revealed if I grouped this text with others that have opposing messages?

› How will I ask students to track their thinking throughout this unit so that they can surface their own questions and formulate answers supported by evidence at the end?

A lot of this initial work is brainwork, testing and discarding your own theories and questions. As you think about grouping texts as a means of grappling with big questions or testing theories, don't be too quick to land on the question or problem at hand. Talk with colleagues about the richness and depth of the questions you're developing. Make sure they are not focus questions, those that have definitive answers.

Investigating Local Issues

There's nothing more compelling to young adults than a local issue, something they can actually see and feel. Sara Dolloff and Fred Carstens are ninth-grade teachers at Tapestry High School in Buffalo, New York, who believe in involving their students in making a difference in their community. Sara and Fred design curriculum for their students that helps the kids understand that, even though they are young adolescents, they can read, write, listen, and speak to have a real impact, provided they take the time to do it well. For example, after reading and discussing case studies of historical reformers such as Martin Luther in Fred's Global Studies class, Sara began having her students think about the power of an individual or a small group of individuals to change dominant institutions.

Tapestry is located in the heart of an economically challenged city, and its students count on (and are somewhat at the mercy of) the regional transportation service for bussing to and from school, including after school when most students practice or play sports or are involved in extracurricular activities. But the schedule of the buses that serviced the school did not readily meet the needs of the students. Through reading and interviews, the students learned how the transportation authority was structured and how it made decisions about bus routes and schedules. The students interviewed bus riders, and they studied the need for and support of public transportation in their community. They formulated plans for change that could work within the necessary financial confines. They examined models of arguments in writing, and then developed compelling letters in which they attempted to convince the transportation authority to improve bus service to the school, citing examples of how it could be done. They presented their arguments at a press conference as well. As of this writing, according to their website, the transportation authority's planning manager has pledged to work with the school to improve its bussing services for the students.

The Tapestry students *wanted* to read about the little guys who took on big institutions and won, because they *were* the little guys. An investigation into the ways a regional transportation authority operates doesn't seem at all interesting from the outside, but if you're trying to get home from after-school sports every day and are reliant on non-existent public transportation to do it, it's pretty relevant. Like the boys profiled in *Reading Don't Fix No Chevys*, Tapestry's freshmen were more likely to be engaged when their literacy work had a purpose.

"Right," you may be saying, "but my town doesn't have a regional transportation authority." OK. But I bet you won't have to look very hard to find the local issues that your students care about. In fact, young adults seem to get pretty fired up about some commonly found broad categories of issue—injustices, local problems, and community improvement. What would your students want to know about:

> The concentration of poverty in a certain geographic area. How does this happen? What are the impacts? What can *we* do?

> Access to health care for children. What are the long-term effects of early-childhood health care? Who doesn't get it? Why? What can *we* do?

> Homelessness. Who are the homeless, really? What can be done? What can *we* do?

> Immigration. Who comes to our town? Why? How are they welcomed and supported (or not)? What can *we* do?

> Natural resources. What (stream, lake, wetland, wilderness) is worth preserving in our town? Is it preserved? If not, why not? What would it take to get it preserved? Could *we* preserve it?

> The state of the school lunch program. Who decides what kids eat at lunch and why? What are the effects? Could *we* change it?

> How much energy does a school (or school district) use, and therefore how much money does it spend on electricity and heat versus learning materials? Can *we* shed light on this? Can *we* make specific recommendations for change?

> What would it take to economically stimulate our (crossroads, main street, city center)? Can *we* campaign for this?

There's a strong motivational link between doing the reading and research required to learn about these issues and the writing and presentation that students do to try to make a change. It's not unusual for students whose schools develop this kind of contextualized curriculum to share their work in order to inform or persuade a public audience outside of the school. For example, the students at Casco Bay High School in Portland, Maine, actually study the patterns of immigration that bring new citizens to their city. In addition to reading and researching human rights issues worldwide that cause people to leave their homes and seek American citizenship, Casco Bay's tenth graders interview immigrants about their experiences and photograph them as well. The students then write profiles of "their" immigrants and use a local gallery to share their powerful writing and often haunting photographs. The work is unveiled at a gallery "opening" where the students and the immigrants share their stories of challenge and renewed hope for the public.

Designing units contextualized by local issues almost always means that teachers need to step out of the school box and into the community themselves. Teachers who do this kind of work often partner with local organizations and experts, well in advance of actually teaching the unit to students. If there's a local issue that you and your students care about and want to learn more about, ask the following questions to help give your unit substance and shape:

> › Who is already working on this issue in our community?
> › What do those people read and write about in their work?
> › What additional information will my students need in order to deeply understand this issue? Where can that information be found? (Librarians are amazing and often underutilized assets in our schools.)
> › What literature is available that enlightens this issue?
> › How can students be authentically involved in helping others to understand and make decisions about this issue?
> › Who is the audience for the students' work?

Exploring Local History

Another way to create context is to engage students through the study of local history. The students from Central Alternative High School in Dubuque, Iowa, studied World War II through the lens of its impact on local veterans. In this case, the cake was the generic social studies standards related to World War II, along with the reading, writing, and speaking skills that students would develop by reading textbooks and primary sources, and reading, writing about, and discussing Joseph Heller's *Catch-22*. The local veterans—their experiences and emotions—were the frosting. As part of this project, after reading extensively to prepare, students conducted interviews with the veterans, asking them to share personal accounts of their experiences in war. The students wrote a book that documented these experiences, combining information about World War II with quotes from the veterans themselves. The book, called *A Tribute to History*, was of such high quality that it was sold in local bookstores. Perhaps more importantly, it honored and personalized the sacrifices made by these students' own community members.

Do you think these students felt a sense of purpose? You bet. There's a second benefit as well; the broader and more public an audience is for students' literacy work, the more engaged, focused, and committed to quality the students become. Contextualizing reading and writing through local topics and issues eliminates the "why do we have to do this?" question. A public, authentic audience for their work drives students toward such high levels of quality that those receiving the finished products are often stunned to find that it is the work of students rather than professionals.

There are many schools and networks of schools in which students routinely read, write, listen, and speak to solve real problems and tackle real issues like these. Expeditionary Learning Schools (www.elschools.org) maintains a public online library of the student work that results from this kind of investigation. I suggest starting there to get your juices flowing. Students in the High Tech High network in California solve problems using math and science skills, along with literacy skills (www.hightechhigh.org). Great sources of ideas for this approach to curriculum include the Buck Institute for Education (www.bie.org) and Edutopia (www.edutopia.org).

One caution about contextualizing curriculum this way; the core of the work must be *literacy* focused in order for teachers to maintain meeting the Common Core Standards. It's not that these projects can't live in social studies or science classrooms and be mostly content focused, they can. But if the project exempts students from reading complex texts and/or doing rigorous writing, students may be deeply engaged in a long-term process that does not address the Common Core Standards. If you choose to design this kind of work for your students, and I hope you do, ensure that many of the learning targets you establish are aligned with the Common Core Standards. Also, be sure you use solid, formative assessment practices to verify that students are growing as readers, writers, listeners, and speakers. For more on learning targets, see Chapter 3.

Much like units designed around local issues, units that dig into local history often require connections to the broader community. Preparing students to interview community members is a particular responsibility when engaging them in community-based studies. Ask yourself:

> What do my students need to know to make the most of the time they have with community members or using community resources?

> What can my students read in order to obtain this essential background knowledge?

> What can my students read and discuss in order to develop a sense of wonder and respect for the development of our community and its citizens over time?

> How can I help my students, perhaps through complex primary sources, grapple with the impact of historical events on the people who lived through them?

> What do my students need to know about developing the questions they will ask? About efficient and effective note taking?

> What practice should my students have so that they are articulate and impressive during this experience?

Examining Ideas from Multiple Perspectives

Another flavor of frosting to consider is the cognitive challenge that comes from deliberately pairing texts that represent multiple perspectives on a historical event or many sides of an issue. This approach is particularly effective when the ideas being explored relate to injustice or inhumanity, or when they reveal uncertainty around situations that people have "always believed happened a certain way." An example of this approach might be to pair Laura Hillenbrand's excellent book *Unbroken*, which tells the almost-impossible-to-believe but true story of a World War II pilot who crashed in the ocean and survived at sea for forty-seven days, only to be captured by the Japanese and tortured for years as a POW, with selections from Jeanne Watatsuki Houston's *Farwell to Manzanar* and primary sources related to both Pearl Harbor and the Japanese Internment Camps. Students could read these texts to grapple with the questions "Who tells the story, the author or the narrator?" and "Do the ends justify the means?"

Here are some other ideas to spark your thinking in this direction:

Text Sets Reflecting Multiple Perspectives	Possible Essential Questions
Eric Schlosser's *Chew on This: Everything You Don't Want to Know About Fast Food* paired with websites from McDonald's, Wendy's, and the like, along with materials from farming movements such as free-range chickens	Is it persuasion or manipulation? Are my nuggets worth the cost?
Wolfgang W. E. Samuel's *German Boy* and John Boyne's *The Boy in the Striped Pajamas*, along with primary sources related to the lives of Jewish children and non-Jewish children in Germany during World War II.	Which impacts the reader more, allegory or reality? What role does innocence play in protecting children from horrific events?

Developing multiple-perspective units can start with your taking a close look at the texts you already teach and thinking about what might represent the "other side" of it. For example, if you teach Tim O'Brien's *The Things They Carried*, research the impact of the Vietnam war on the Vietnamese children or the long-term impact of being a conscientious objector during that time. If you believe that the essence of *The Catcher in the Rye* is the universality of Holden Caulfield's rather sulky quest for identity, add excerpts from Pipher and Ross's *Reviving Ophelia* (2005), articles about self-concept and identity, and then read

Betty Smith's *A Tree Grows in Brooklyn* for contrast. Notice I am recommending that *you*, the teacher, do this work before you bring it to your students. Creating compelling contextualized curriculum means that *you* have to be compelled by the context. Without your passion and excitement about taking students along on a journey, context falls flat.

Another key aspect of helping students make sense of texts that represent multiple perspectives is that you yourself have to suspend a bias toward one side or another. If students feel that there is a perspective that's "right" in your classroom, they won't attend carefully to all the texts. It's important that you read deeply yourself into the texts that represent the "other side," thinking carefully about what students might say about those texts and how you will create space for their responses. Be prepared to:

> Use protocols for discussion, so that all students have opportunities to test out and support their opinions. This is the heart of Common Core College and Career Readiness Anchor Standards for Speaking and Listening 1, which says students will "Prepare for and participate effectively in a range of conversations and collaborations with diverse partners, building on others' ideas and expressing their own clearly and persuasively." The National School Reform Faculty website has a huge collection of protocols that can be modified for any age group. (www.nsrfharmony.org/protocols.html). In modeling this work for teachers, I have come to rely on Stephen Brookfield and Stephen Preskill's book *Discussion as a Way of Teaching: Tools and Techniques for Democratic Classrooms,* updated in 2005.

> Set "ground rules," or norms, for discussion in your classroom, teaching students that it is perfectly fine to disagree with each other as long as their responses are respectful. Teach the difference between respectful disagreement and disrespectful disagreement.

> Honor the thinking of the students whose views don't match your own, while still being sure that students use evidence from the text to support their responses.

Analyzing Mentor Texts

Some texts are compelling both because of the stories they tell and the way they are told. These texts often disrupt traditions—they are nonlinear, or incorporate subtexts in new and different ways, or feature a narrator with an unusual voice. Sets of these kinds of texts can serve as "mentors"—showing students how to break literary rules in ways that make readers sit up and take notice. In this case, it is the author's craft that becomes the context.

I have long been a fan of Mark Haddon's *The Curious Incident of the Dog in the Night-Time*. The story is not just about a boy on the autism spectrum, it is told *by* that boy. His voice, while purposefully somewhat expressionless, is so unusual and darned interesting. When I read that book, and I have about twelve times, I think about all the other unusual voices that could tell stories in new and different ways. Garth Stein's *The Art of Racing the Rain* is told by a dog (there are actually many books and stories told by cats and dogs). *The Book Thief*, by Marcus Zusak, is narrated by death personified. Alice Sebold's *The Lovely Bones* is told by a girl who has died. Studying these kinds of texts really pushes readers to think about narrators as constructs of the author, created to bring something specific to the story. Texts like these beg to be read closely, and new-forming authors itch to try the techniques they're observing. When we create context for challenging texts by studying powerful examples of craft, we motivate both the reading and writing places in our students' brains.

Here are a few other ideas for text sets that teach something specific about the author's craft. Hopefully this list gets you thinking about many more possibilities:

Sets of Potential Mentor Texts	Aspect of Craft	Possible Essential Questions
"A Sense of Place" *The Lord of the Rings*, J. R. R. Tolkien *The Secret Garden*, Frances Hogdson Burnett *The Road*, Cormac McCarthy *The Handmaid's Tale*, Margaret Atwood	Setting	How does a reader "see" the setting? Does a story happen in a place or because of a place?
"The Subtle Argument" *The Immortal Life of Henrietta Lacks*, Rebecca Skloot *Nickel and Dimed*, Barbara Ehrenreich	Argument	Are facts or people more compelling? What's more powerful, showing or telling?
"Every Word Counts" *The Preamble to the United States Constitution* "The Gettysburg Address," Abraham Lincoln "Blood, Toil, Tears and Sweat," Winston Churchill "The Whiskey Speech," Noah S. Sweat	Word Choice	Is there such a thing as the "wrong word?" Does the struggle for precision pay off?

Designing units that illuminate craft through text sets helps ensure that students meet the Common Core Standards for Literature 4–6, 9, and 10. These particular standards have specific grade-level variations that demand that literature be grouped and examined in this way. For example, grades 11–12 Standard 5 requires that students "Analyze how an author's choices concerning how to structure specific parts of a text (e.g., the choice of where to begin or end a story, the choice to provide a comedic or tragic resolution) contribute to its overall structure and meaning as well as its aesthetic impact." Although this can be done while reading one text, students' thinking will be richer and higher-order if they compare and contrast the way it's done through at least parts of multiple texts. The same is true of grade 7, Standard 9: "Compare and contrast a fictional portrayal of a time, place, or character and a historical account of the same period as a means of understanding how authors of fiction use or alter history." A unit focused on this standard must offer students the opportunity to deeply understand both a historical period and the way authors craft fiction based on history. Again, students can do that once, with one text, but they will be all the stronger as both readers and writers if they discover patterns across texts and come to discover the intentionality of each author's work.

When working to create a compelling context through author's craft, ask yourself:

> What does this author do differently than anyone else my students have studied?

> How can I highlight this technique by showing other models, or help my students analyze it by seeing the same techniques handled in different ways?

> What opportunities will my students have to copy these masters in service of developing their own craft?

The Challenge of Context plus Complexity

There are likely hundreds of other ways to wrap challenging texts in context, or to frost the standards cake. You may already be thinking of your own ideas. But whether you try one of the methods from this chapter or devise your own, you must keep your eyes on the prize of selecting and providing texts that are both compelling *and* complex. Without much practice with complex texts within each unit of curriculum, we will lose the promise of the Common Core Standards—to prepare all students for college and careers. Our students must be engaged, yes, but in service of working hard to understand what a text is offering them.

Defining complexity is, in and of itself, complex. Appendix A of the Common Core Standards for English Language Arts and Literacy in History/Social Studies, Science, and Technical Subjects and its supplement clarify that text complexity is defined through a relationship between the text, the reader, and the task—all of which vary greatly.

Appendix A suggests that teachers and others concerned with defining text complexity consider the following aspects:

> › *Qualitative dimensions and factors.* These have to do with the meaning of texts, the sophistication of the content and themes, the conventionality of the structures and language, and the newness of the content to the reader.

> › *Quantitative dimensions and factors.* This is often known as the "readability" of a text and has to do with the syntax, average sentence length, and the frequency of demanding vocabulary. Qualitative factors are often measured by computer programs such as those created by MetaMetrics (Lexiles), Degrees of Reading Power, and Flesch-Kincaid, teachers can access easily and for free if their computers include Microsoft Word (turn on the "readability statistics").

> › *Reader and task factors.* This dimension of complexity relies on teachers knowing their students and their awareness of the tasks they are asking readers to complete. Some challenged readers have tremendous capacity to persevere through difficult texts; others need support to develop that mindset. When a task is very complex, perhaps students are best served by accessing less complex text in order to complete the task. This aspect of complexity relies on teachers' true professional judgment.

One place where the Common Core Standards are very explicit is the complexity "band," *based on qualitative measures only*, expected at each grade level. The chart on the next page is a helpful starting place for determining whether a text is complex enough for readers at your grade level to cut their teeth on.

It's really important, though, to remember that quantitative measures alone do not tell the whole story of a text's complexity. Earlier I mentioned the novel *The Book Thief*, which is a perfect example of the potential conflict between quantitative and qualitative measures of complexity. *The Book Thief* has a 730 Lexile measure, which makes it appropriate— quantitatively—for second or third grade. But the book is about the Holocaust, and the unconventionality of its narrator makes it much more complex than its Lexile measure alone suggests. It's definitely an upper middle school or lower high school book, and teachers should take care to engage students deeply in the analysis of the author's choice to personify death as a literary technique, to ensure full access to the complexity this text offers. The

Lexile measures of *The Grapes of Wrath* (680L) and *The Red Pony* (810L) speak more to Steinbeck's use of straightforward syntax than to the complexity of his themes. The same holds true for Hemingway's *The Old Man and the Sea* (910L).

Grades	Lexile	ATOS	DRP	FK	SR	RM
6–8	925–1185	7.00–9.98	57–67	6.51–10.34	4.11–10.66	7.04–9.57
9–10	1050–1335	9.67–12.01	62–72	8.32–12.12	9.02–13.93	8.41–10.81
11–CCR	1185–1385	11.20–14.10	67–74	10.34–14.2	12.30–14.50	9.57–12

Lexile	Lexile (MetaMetrics)
ATOS	Accelerated Reader (Renaissance Learning)
DRP	Degrees of Reading Power (Questar)
FK	Flesch-Kincaid
SR	Source Rater (Educational Testing Service)
RM	Pearson Reading Maturity Metric (Pearson Education)

Source: Supplement to Appendix A of the Common Core Standards.

On the flip side, there are many books that are commonly taught, particularly in middle schools, that students and teachers enjoy greatly but that don't require *teaching* so much as they require *offering*. Suzanne Collins' *The Hunger Games* is a great example of this kind of book. The plot leaves you breathless, it has well-developed characters that you come to know and care about (or hate), and readers can literally see the fog creeping into the arena and hear the booming of the canon. It's vivid but straightforward. Its Lexile measure is 810, which means lots and lots of kids, even struggling readers, can make great sense of it and enjoy it *all on their own*, or with friends. It should not be the basis of a curriculum that's attempting to stretch readers every day so that they are college and career ready.

Qualitative measures that teachers should consider when determining a texts' complexity include:

Structure. Some texts work in an orderly or straightforward structure, such as beginning to end in chronological order. Others are made more complex, for example through the use of multiple flashbacks, or by integrating narrative text into an informational piece.

Language Conventionality and Clarity. Texts whose meaning is couched in a great deal of figurative language or jargon, for example, are more complex than texts that use straightforward language.

Knowledge Demands. Texts that presume the reader has a great deal of background knowledge are much more complex than texts that teach or reveal as the reader reads along.

Levels of Meaning or Purpose. Literary texts whose themes are clear and straightforward are less complex than texts with obscure themes. Informational texts that clearly teach, explain, or argue are simpler than informational texts whose purpose is not clear.

One last thought on complex text. According to Appendix A of the Common Core Standards, there's a great deal of research behind the push to use it, not the least of which is the roughly 350 Lexile point difference between the texts students are currently reading as high school seniors and what they are expected to read upon entering college or the workforce (p. 3). However, that does not mean that complex text is all that students should be allowed or encouraged to read. Earlier, I mentioned Suzanne Collins' *The Hunger Games* as an example of a text that's not complex, based on either quantitative or qualitative measures for most middle and high school students. But it should be handed out like candy in middle schools, literally given as a gift, to show kids that books can be just as entertaining as television, movies, and video games. If we are to achieve the promise of the Common Core Standards, we need to both hook students on books they will simply consume and read with joy, with the "buzz" that comes with discovering a book that literally transports you into the lives of characters you wish you knew personally, *and* on contextualized complex reading that we will guide them through with great tenacity. Complex text should be the basis for schools' curricula and the core of compelling, contextualized units. Other texts still have a place in schools—in book clubs, in independent reading programs, in summer reading, and the like. But where there are teachers to guide students, there should be complex text at hand. When students are reading on their own, they should be encouraged to read anything they find appealing.

Finding Complex Yet Compelling Texts

When I work with teachers, they often ask me where I get the ideas for all of my units. The charts in this chapter come from my life as a reader. If we are going to turn students on to complex texts, we need to be turned on by complex texts ourselves. I read everything now with an eye for context. I ask myself, "If I were going to teach this, what would I do with it?" "What can I combine it with and why?" "What could I help the kids notice?" I can't think of a simple way around this, and frankly, I hope there isn't one. If we are going to ask our students to really grapple with a text, we'd better be willing to do the same.

That being said, there are resources and websites that can help you decide what to read in order to prepare contextualized curriculum for your students. In many schools, the Library Media Specialist is vastly underutilized. My experience with these specialists is that they very much want to be more involved in the conversation about what books, other texts, and other media students can and should be accessing. If I were in charge of such things, Library Media Specialists would be released from the library regularly to share planning time with classroom teachers. Simply having them sit in on planning conversations would likely result in more students engaged in more complex and compelling texts more often.

Each year, the American Library Association publishes lists of books, graphic novels, audiobooks, and films for young adults. These lists include excellent descriptions, and I have often discovered new things to read through their recommendations. You can see the lists, going back to 1996, by visiting: www.ala.org/yalsa/booklists/bbya, and for the most recent Best Fiction for Young Adults lists, visit: www.ala.org/yalsa/bfya.

The *New York Times* has created a free section of its website specifically for educators, a blog called The Learning Network, that features great read-alouds and that pairs *New York Times* articles with novels and poems in really interesting ways: http://learning.blogs. nytimes.com. For example, a search for *The Great Gatsby* offers the following resources from the *New York Times* archives: F. Scott Fitzgerald's obituary, links to primary sources from his life, an article about young people searching for the American dream, a 1925 book review of *The Great Gatsby*, and more.

Goodreads (www.goodreads.com) is an amazing website for readers that seems to work on the same principles as Pandora does for music. You find and rate books that you love, like, or hate, and Goodreads guides you toward more books that you might love, like, or hate. I noted on Goodreads that I liked Jeannette Walls' *The Glass Castle* and it turned me on to Rick Bragg's *All Over but the Shoutin'*, which I am thoroughly enjoying. I have a list of books (fifty-four actually) started because of Goodreads. You can see what your friends are reading, review books, write book reviews, see others' reviews, and with one click, purchase books you just have to have.

I stalk the Top Ten lists people post on Amazon, and often find myself standing in bookstores, trailing my hands lovingly over covers, I constantly bring conversations back to "What are you reading right now?" I'm forever losing myself in Internet trails that end up in obscure places like libraryzest.blogspot.com. Gary Paulsen once recommended that we should "read like a wolf eats." I wonder if wolves like frosting?

Keys to Help You Make This Critical Move

> If we are going to help students meet the challenge of complex text, we can't ask them to read for the sake of reading. We can't talk about teaching in terms of units titled by names of books, as in "my *Outsiders* unit," "my *Red Badge of Courage* unit," or the "short stories" unit.

> Units based on single novels sideline the importance of nonfiction, a critical aspect of the shifts required by the Common Core Standards.

> Curriculum can be contextualized in multiple ways, but in order to meet the Common Core Standards, reading complex texts must be a regular means of learning and discussing.

> Text complexity is based on quantitative and qualitative factors.

> Students should be allowed and encouraged to read other texts purely for enjoyment.

> To be teachers of complex texts, we must be avid and engaged readers of complex texts.

Works Cited

Common Core State Standards for English Language Arts and Literacy in History/Social Studies, Science, and Technical Studies: Appendix A. Available online: www.corestandards.org/assets/Appendix_A.pdf

Smith, Michael, and Jeffrey D. Wilhelm. 2002. *Reading Don't Fix No Chevys: Literacy in the Lives of Young Men*. Portsmouth, NH: Heinemann.

Wiggins, Grant, and Jay McTighe. 2005. *Understanding by Design*. Expanded 2nd Edition. Alexandria, VA: ASCD.

CHAPTER THREE

DEVELOP STUDENT-SHARED GOALS

How Historians Read

Rich Richardson is a middle school social studies teacher at a public middle school for at-risk students in the city of Syracuse, New York. Social studies teachers offer some of the most complex and interesting texts students encounter—primary source documents shaped by their authors' points of view, and secondary sources that assume the reader has vast background knowledge. Even textbooks, the mainstay of many social studies classrooms, can be interesting and they are certainly complex. Critical readers of textbooks consider what has been included and what hasn't. Helping students tackle these texts can bring history to life, but many teachers find their students so challenged by these texts that they give up and talk about them instead.

Historians read primary and secondary sources in deep and analytical ways. They consider individual words, phrases, and entire documents in terms of what they say, what they don't say, and how they say it. Historians decide whether primary sources reflect the times in which they were developed and the authors who wrote them or whether they stand in contrast to the expected. They allow one document to lead them to another. They glean the small details within the context of big ideas. They read other historians' claims and pick their arguments apart, sourced evidence by sourced evidence. Historians read to make meaning of times and events long ago and far away. Rich wants his students to be historians.

Rich and his colleagues believe that one of the most significant aspects of their students' success is the school's commitment to formative assessment strategies that lead to students *owning* their learning goals—many of which have to do with the skills they need to read and build their background knowledge as historians.

Where Student-Shared Learning Targets Come From

The work of creating student-shared goals through formative assessment practices begins with creating clarity around exactly what students are expected to learn in any given learning experience. This clarity can come through the development of standards-aligned "I can" statements, what Rick Stiggins calls "learning targets" (2012). You might have noticed the "I can" statements, or learning targets, in the Holocaust unit plan in Chapter 1. Unlike objectives, which teachers often develop to guide their own thinking about what it is students are expected to know, understand, and be able to do, learning targets are intended for *students* to use, in conjunction with the teacher, in order to understand both their long-term and daily learning goals. Students co-construct with teachers a plan for meeting those goals and tracking their progress. These student-shared goals help engage, support, and hold students accountable for tackling curriculum, for the careful reading of complex texts, and for sharing their understanding through speaking and writing.

As an example, one of Rich's most powerful units is "The Progress Dilemma," through which his eighth-grade students consider the positive and negative impacts of the rapid social, political, technological, and environmental changes that have occurred worldwide in the last 100 years. As students learn about these changes, they read texts such as Rachel Carson's *Silent Spring*, Howard Zinn's *A People's History of the United States*, the memoirs of the Little Rock Nine, the accounts of astronauts, documents and reports related to the environmental cleanup of their city's local Onondaga Lake, and statistics related to the distribution of wealth in America. Rich knows his students have to read these things closely to gather evidence to answer the question, "Is progress good?" Although his ELA colleague is also working on students' reading skills, Rich has accepted the responsibility of *also* helping his students to meet the challenge of complex text.

Developing learning targets starts with a deep understanding of the standards students are expected to achieve. In Rich's state of New York, the social studies standards are organized into key ideas that define the essential and enduring understandings that students should achieve. Rich knows his students must come to understand the following ideas from the *content* of his course:

> After World War I, there was a great deal of innovation and many Americans became more prosperous. Some did not, however.

> A nearly 40-year clash between the United States and the Soviet Union was known as the Cold War.

> Life in America was impacted by the Cold War in many ways.

> A powerful time of change in America was the Civil Rights movement. It occurred during the 1950s–60s and lead to changes in African American rights. The discussion of equal rights for women and other groups continues today.

> Many domestic and global challenges face America today, including terrorism, environmental concerns, and increased economic competition and interdependence.[1]

But Rich's study of what he will teach his students does not end with content. Rich knows that in order for his students to come to understand history deeply, they will need to be critical readers, as real historians are. In order to show what they understand, the students will ultimately write an argument in which they take a stand on the question, "Is progress good?" So Rich also examines the Common Core Standards for Literacy in History/Social Studies, Science, and Technical Subjects as guidance for the kind of teaching he needs to do with complex text. He determines that he will focus on the following Common Core Literacy Standards as he works with his students in this particular learning expedition:

> Cite specific textual evidence to support analysis of primary and secondary sources.

> Determine the central ideas or information of a primary or secondary source; provide an accurate summary of the source, distinct from prior knowledge or opinions.

> Determine the meaning of words and phrases as they are used in a text, including vocabulary specific to domains related to history/social studies.

> Identify aspects of a text that reveal an author's point of view or purpose (e.g., loaded language, inclusion, or avoidance of particular facts).

> Write arguments focused on discipline-specific content.

I have been in classrooms where standards like those above are posted and even referred to with students. But the thing about these types of standards is that they were written for

---

[1]At the time of this writing, more specific ideas were in draft form, released for public comment at the New York State K-8 Common Core Social Studies Framework.

teachers, not students. It's hard to get students involved in goals that do not seem relevant to them and that they possibly don't understand. Furthermore, the standards listed in this example are generic; they do not reflect the context in which the students might be working on them.

Learning targets are not simple restatements of standards, they are designed to be student-friendly so that learners come to develop a clear vision of what they are expected to accomplish. In this way, teachers invite students into *learning* rather than *doing*. Students move from passive receivers of tasks to complete (or not), to active decision makers. What is expected of me? How can I get there? Have I gotten there? An effective learning target helps students to:

> › understand and be able to communicate effectively about the specific learning goals they are expected to master

> › develop a vision for what it looks like to be successful

> › track their own progress so that they own their goals and develop a sense of efficacy. Efficacy can come both by being successful or by being initially unsuccessful but then overcoming a challenge.

Once Rich determines which standards he will meet in any given learning experience, he translates them into language that his students will understand. This first set of targets, those based specifically on the standards, are *long-term targets* as they are sometimes the culmination of several weeks or months of work. Here are some examples of both content and literacy long-term targets from Rich's work:

Standards	Long-Term Targets
Understand how the United States and other societies develop economic systems and associated institutions to allocate scarce resources, how major decision-making units function in the U.S. and other national economies, and how an economy solves the scarcity problem through market and nonmarket mechanisms. (New York State Learning Standards for Social Studies 1996)	I can describe the aspects of progress that led to prosperity for many people in the 1920s. I can analyze the reasons why all Americans did not benefit from the aspects of progress that many people experienced in 1920s.
Cite specific textual evidence to support analysis of primary and secondary sources.	I can fluently read materials related to the progress dilemma. I can use specific details to explain the meaning of the things I read about the progress dilemma.
Determine the central ideas or information of a primary or secondary source; provide an accurate summary of the source, distinct from prior knowledge or opinions.	I can determine the central ideas, or most important information, in the things I read about the progress dilemma. I can accurately summarize the things I read about the progress dilemma.
Write arguments focused on discipline-specific content.	I can develop an effective argument regarding whether or not progress is good.

Creating and Organizing a Variety of Targets

Stiggins notes that learning targets fall into a variety of categories (2012). Some targets reflect content mastery and help determine what students should be able to do when they have acquired that mastery. In this case, Rich wants his students to know the "aspects of progress" that led to progress well enough to *describe* them.

Some targets reflect specific underlying skills that students are to develop, skills that enable students to participate in the process of learning. In this case, Rich is working with students on the underlying skill of reading *fluently*. Fluent reading is not an end game, however. It's a skill that works in service of higher-order thinking, or reasoning, wherein the learner uses his or her knowledge and foundational skills to solve a problem or figure something out. Many of the Common Core Standards for reading are reasoning targets and therefore reflect the students' need to think, problem solve, and comprehend through analysis and inference.

In this case, Rich wants his students to *determine* and *summarize* central ideas. Another set of targets have to do with the products students create to synthesize or show their learning. Rich wants his students to *develop* a product, an *effective argument*.

As Stiggins suggests, Rich carefully chooses the verbs in his learning targets to reflect whether students are acquiring knowledge, developing skills, reasoning, or creating a product.

Knowledge	Performance/Skill	Reasoning	Product
I can describe the changes that led to prosperity for many people in the 1920s.	I can fluently read materials related to the progress dilemma.	I can determine the central ideas, or most important information, of the things I read about the progress dilemma.	I can develop an effective argument regarding whether or not progress is good.
		I can analyze the reasons why all Americans did not benefit from the economic boom of the 1920s.	

By creating a set of long-term targets that reflect both content and literacy skills and reasoning, Rich shows his students that their goals related to learning content are as important as their goals related to reading and writing well. This is an important message for Rich to send to his students in regard to their learning. It says to them that part of being a good social studies student is being a good reader and an effective writer. This clear expectation in content-area classrooms means that students are more likely to tackle the challenge of complex text throughout the day, not just in English Language Arts.

Creating Targets and Matched Assessments

The next step for Rich, often with the support of his ELA colleagues, is to create a roadmap that helps him stay focused on helping his students both learn content and develop their literacy skills. This roadmap is also used intentionally to help students understand the smaller steps they will take in order to master the long-term target. Rich goes about developing this roadmap in two ways, not necessarily in order. One way is to analyze the tasks his students will likely be completing over the course of the learning. For example, Rich has his students keep a Central Idea/Supporting Details T-chart when reading. Rich thinks about, "What will my students need to know in order to complete these T-charts? What skills do they need to have? What reasoning will they need to apply?" Another way Rich develops a roadmap is to envision the assessment of the target. He wonders "How will students show that they have mastered this target? What will they know, understand, and be able to do?" This thinking leads to a cohesive set of *supporting targets* and assessments, which are related to the smaller chunks of learning that accumulate in evidence of mastery of the long-term target. Here's an example from Rich's work, specifically as it relates to his students' reading of complex text:

Long-Term Targets	Supporting Targets	Assessments
I can determine the central ideas, or most important information, of the things I read about the progress dilemma.	I can define the term "central idea." I can explain the difference between the common position of central ideas in textbooks vs. primary source documents. I can read and re-read material related to the progress dilemma to develop fluency. I can read material related to the progress dilemma and identify one or more central idea(s). I can re-read material related to the progress dilemma, looking for specific details that support the central idea(s).	**Formative:** Notebook check (definition of central idea). Fluency check. "Gist" statements from in-class reading. Central Idea/Supporting Details T-charts from in-class reading and homework. **Summative:** Students will independently read a passage from *A People's History of the United States* that they have not worked on in class or for homework and complete a Central Idea/Supporting Details T-chart.
I can accurately summarize the things I read about the progress dilemma.	I can define the characteristics of an accurate summary. I can read material related to the progress dilemma and identify one or more central idea(s). I can re-read material related to the progress dilemma looking for specific details that support the central idea(s). I can develop a summary of each central idea in material I read about the progress dilemma.	**Formative:** Notebook check (characteristics of summary). "Gist" statements. Central idea/detail t-charts. Practice summaries. **Summative:** Students will independently read a passage from *A People's History of the United States* that they have not worked on in class or for homework and develop a summary.

(A similar example of a Standards-Targets-Assessment plan is found in Chapter 1, in the exemplar Holocaust unit that Michelle and Paul developed.)

Notice how Rich plans at this stage for both formative assessments that will lead to practice, feedback, and more practice during learning experiences, and summative assessments that he will use to benchmark students' performance so that he, they, and their parents know if they are doing as expected.

According to Moss and Brookhart (2012), it is the careful crafting and use of the lesson-sized learning targets—the roadmap that comes from determining the supporting targets—that has the most impact on student learning. Creating a very thoughtful set of supporting targets invariably leads to aha moments for teachers about what their students will need to learn, and, therefore, what they should plan to teach. In Rich's case, he hadn't thought about needing to be sure his students know what a central idea is or if they understand the characteristics of an effective summary prior to developing his chart. Like many secondary teachers, he presumed his students knew those things. Some of them do, but not all of them. Planning smarter and not harder involves planning to check for gaps, so that they can be addressed. Remember, strong formative assessment practices raise achievement for all students, but they help struggling students most of all.

Daily Structures to Ensure That Students Understand and Use the Targets

Once Rich has developed his long-term and supporting targets—and he double-checks that he has created both content-focused and literacy-focused targets—he begins planning for the time and the tools he will use to engage his students in the formative assessment process. The obvious way is to share and discuss the targets with students, but that alone does bring students into the process deeply enough to truly turn targets into student-shared goals. So Rich also plans to:

> ask students to restate the targets in their own words

> ask students to pre-assess themselves related to the targets and let him know where they think they are going to make the most growth

> ask students if they think there are targets that are missing and add the targets they think they will need

> frequently ask students to label their work with the target it is designed to address.

This particular set of formative assessment strategies can be done by a creating a chart like the one below, and by providing time and support for students to complete it. Completing it is a multi-step process that begins with students discussing the targets with the teacher and each other (sometimes teachers even use pictures and models to help students understand the target). Then students rewrite the learning targets in their own words, putting the date or a symbol in each of the levels of proficiency at the top to indicate where they believe they are before the learning begins, and perhaps, adding additional targets that they feel the need to learn in order to master the long-term target. Skills that students work on over time in increasingly sophisticated contexts, like the skills involved in reading complex texts, are worth checking in on before additional practice. Pre-assessment like this, when combined with teachers' knowledge of their students' needs based on ongoing work samples, forms the basis of effective differentiation. This is discussed more deeply in Chapter 5.

Learning-Targets Tracker					
Have Mastered This					
Pretty Good					
Just Beginning					
In My Words					
Supporting Targets	I can define the term "central idea."	I can explain the difference between the common position of central ideas in textbooks vs. primary source documents.	I can read and re-read material related to the progress dilemma to develop fluency.	I can read material related to the progress dilemma and identify one or more central idea(s).	I can re-read material related to the progress dilemma, looking for specific details that support the central idea(s).
Long-Term Target	I can determine the central ideas, or most important information, of the things I read about the progress dilemma.				

As the learning experience unfolds, students later return to this chart, which they call a "tracker," and indicate where they think they are as the work progresses, by considering the work they have completed and Rich's feedback. They add a new date or a different symbol in the box that represents their most recent proficiency. In this way, both the students and the teacher have an ongoing sense of how the learning is going. Kids who see themselves moving from "just beginning" to "pretty good" internalize a clear picture of their progress. Kids who started out believing they had "mastered" a skill then perhaps realize that they are only "pretty good," have developed a clearer picture of expectations (this happens often, and it's a good thing!). Kids who linger at "just beginning" become more open to conversations about additional support, the importance of their homework practice, or being more focused in the classroom.

Moving Beyond Tracking

In addition to the steps encapsulated in the tracker, Rich plans to use a variety of other formative assessment strategies over the course of the unit. These strategies fall into the category of helping students develop a vision of what it means to be successful (Stiggins 2012):

> › Ask students to examine models of successful work, sometimes before and often after they make their own attempts.

> › Ask students to help develop criteria for successful work, based on the models they examine.

> › Allow students to revise their work so that they move closer to what's expected.

The "sometimes before and often after" statement in the first bullet above may have caught you by surprise. I have been thinking a great deal about the role of models in the classroom. I do believe that models are extremely important in terms of students' ultimate mastery of a skill. However, I've noticed that when models are introduced early, before students make an attempt at developing their own ideas or products, they tend to stick pretty close to the models. This seems to apply especially to many capable learners, who sometimes worry more about "getting it right" than about the thinking and learning that they are supposed to be doing. When the skill or product is something that students have absolutely no background in—for example, the very first time they write a formal research paper—then up-front models are an important scaffold. But when the skill or product is something students have tried before—such as when writing a summary, to use an example from Rich's work—then sharing and analyzing models *after* students have given it a go leads to more complex thinking from the students. Also, it almost always inspires them to want to revise and improve their work.

In her book *Mindset: The New Psychology of Success* (2006), Carol Dweck describes the beliefs of learners with a growth mindset. Like many of Rich's students, learners with a growth mindset do not perceive "not getting it right the first time" as a setback, but rather as an opportunity to learn more. They do not see their intelligence and abilities as fixed (either I can read this hard stuff or I can't), instead they have the attitude that their effort will lead to success. Although not all learners come to school with a growth mindset, through her research Dweck shows that it can be developed. A growth mindset is the ultimate outcome of learning that's steeped in formative assessment.

The Impact of Clear Targets and Assessments on Student Learning

The time Rich invested in developing student-shared goals comes to fruition early in the unit. It's March, and his students are at the beginning of their Progress Dilemma unit. Students are just beginning to catch on to the idea that many of the relative comforts of their lives come at a potential cost to other people or the environment. Today, they will begin reading about the destruction and cleanup of their city's Onondaga Lake, called by several sources "the most polluted lake in America." Once, the area surrounding Onondaga Lake was the pristine center of the Iroquois Confederacy, but the growth of a major city and surrounding suburbs and the industrialization of the shores of the lake led to years of sewage and chemicals being discharged into the water. Students will read texts from the Department of Environmental Conservation (DEC), from the Onondaga Nation, from the Native American people—who, for years, advocated for restoration of the lake—from the Onondaga Lake Partnership, and from their city and county governments.

"OK, guys, we're going to dive into this stuff," Rich tells his students. "I've looked over your learning-targets trackers, and I know many of you think this reading is going to be complicated. Turn and talk to your neighbor about *what* you think will make it hard." Rich listens as his kids mention things like "lots of technical words" and "long sentences not written for kids."

"You're right about that," he says to the class. "But let's look at our target for today. 'I can explain the difference between the common position of central ideas in primary source documents vs. textbooks.' Who has a good restatement of what that means?"

A student offers clarity on the target, "It's like in textbooks, the central idea is in the first part of the paragraph a lot, but in documents you have to read a lot, maybe the whole thing, before you know what the big ideas are."

"So what does that mean about our work today?" Rich prompts.

"We are going to have to be patient and not rush," another student says, eliciting a few agonized yet friendly groans from classmates. "We are going to have to read the whole thing before we start making decisions about the central ideas."

"That's right, thanks," says Rich. "We are going to start with this one from the DEC because it gives a solid overview of the whole issue. I'm going to read the first page to you aloud, and then you're going to re-read it on your own before we talk about it a bit, OK? By the end of class today, you will have a couple of gist statements from this reading, and I bet you will feel more confident about reading for central ideas."

And off they go, with a noticeable level of commitment to the task.

The next day, Rich shared three gist statements from the class that came close to the mark, along with one that he wrote, which was spot-on. His students analyzed the models and talked about the things they saw that made the statements strong ("it's from the part we read, not just the one part at the top," "it doesn't give too many details, it's a big idea.") As they head into that day's reading, the students are even more confident that they will succeed with their complex text.

Keys to Help You Make This Critical Move

Teachers who plan quality learning targets demystify the outcomes of learning, both for themselves and their students. Targets are the public face of a curriculum, they move what is to be learned out of the curriculum binder and out of teachers' heads, and make the intention of any given learning period public, knowable, and doable. Furthermore, when students reflect on their progress toward targets, like Rich's students do, they *and* their teachers are aware of whether or not they are making the expected progress. Students begin to share a growth mindset that suggests that it is sustained effort that leads to success. The follow-up conversation—celebrating what has been achieved and planning for next steps—ensures that all students are supported and held accountable for their learning.

To recap, planning for student-shared goals to help students meet the challenge of complex text involves:

> starting with the standards, in order to ensure that contextualized curriculum remains focused on essential outcomes

> focusing on both content and literacy standards

> translating standards into student-friendly and contextualized long-term targets

> analyzing tasks and considering what assessments will be used in order to develop a roadmap of supporting targets

> planning the time and opportunity for students to enter into the conversation by asking them to restate, pre-assess, and perhaps identify additional targets

> planning to help students develop a vision of success by strategically offering models and co-constructing criteria for success

> planning time for students to revise their work.

Works Cited

Black, Paul, and Dylan Wiliam. 1998. "Inside the Black Box: Raising Standards Through Classroom Assessment." *Phi Delta Kappan* 80(2): 139–149.

Dweck, Carol. 2006. *Mindset: The New Psychology of Success.* New York, NY: Random House.

Moss, Connie M., and Susan M. Brookhart. 2009. *Advancing Formative Assessment in Every Classroom: A Guide for Instructional Leaders.* Alexandria, VA: Association for Supervision & Curriculum Development.

Moss, Connie M., and Susan M. Brookhart. 2012. *Learning Targets: Helping Students Aim for Understanding in Today's Lesson.* Alexandria, VA: Association for Supervision & Curriculum Development.

Stiggins, Rick J., Judith Arter, Jan Chappuis, and Steve Chappuis. 2012. *Classroom Assessment for Student Learning: Doing It Right—Using It Well.* Portland, OR: Pearson Assessment Training Institute.

CHAPTER FOUR

SELECT STRATEGIES
THAT BUILD UNDERSTANDING

High school biology teacher Mark Louis knows he has to help his students become readers. "There is more science in the world than I could ever tell them about," he explains. "If they can't—or won't—read, they will never really be able to deeply learn science."

Mark is a fan of the vision of literate students found in the introduction of the Common Core standards, particularly the descriptors that refer to students becoming independent builders of content knowledge. According to the CCSS English Language Arts Standards Introduction, students who are college and career ready can, "comprehend and evaluate complex texts across a range of types and disciplines. . . . They become proficient in new areas through research and study. They read purposefully and listen attentively to gain both general knowledge and discipline-specific expertise" (2010). Mark wants that vision to come to life in his classroom.

When I met Mark, he had tried all kinds of things to get his students reading; weekly science articles from newspapers and magazines, quizzes based on textbook reading, websites with amazing photographs and interactive features were all regularly assigned in his course. But he had not been satisfied with the results. "The stronger readers read the assignments," he bemoaned, "but they don't really *think* about what they are reading. They just seem to want to get the answers to the questions, that's it. And the more challenged readers hardly ever try it at all. How do I build these 'independent content learners?'"

Mark was doing a good job with many portions of the up-front stages of planning units that could potentially incorporate complex texts. He envisioned units designed around essential questions that incorporated both the knowledge and skills that scientists employ. He was very clear on how his students would be assessed on their content knowledge and had spent time gathering really interesting texts for his students to read. But reading in his class felt like an "add-on." He knew he wanted to help students become better readers, but he wasn't sure how to get there.

As a science teacher, Mark had never really had the opportunity to learn more about selecting and skillfully using strategies to help his students make meaning from complex texts. He needed to change his practice to incorporate strategies that would help his students learn to read complex texts.

The Problem with Assigning and Assessing

Typically, Mark expected his students to complete assigned reading and a series of questions as part of their homework. This, according to literacy expert Richard Allington, is an instructional paradigm in which many teachers, and secondary teachers in particular, are trapped (2000). Teachers "assign" certain texts to students and then "assess," through a series of questions, whether or not students completed the reading or if they understood it.

Two parts of this paradigm are problematic. First, if a text is genuinely complex (as described in Chapter 2), students need the scaffolds and supports that a teacher will provide in order to fully comprehend it. Students often need the monitoring and encouragement a teacher will provide in order to stick with it. Complex text is meant to be taught, not assigned. Second, developing strategic questions that really drive students into reading and scaffold their understanding of complex text takes—you guessed it—planning.

The comprehension questions found in textbooks or that teachers make up on the fly often work *against* deep reading; students just skim for the answers because that's all the questions ask of them. Many comprehension questions—what used to be called "study guides" when I was in the classroom, as well as those ubiquitous questions at the end of a chapter—are *assessments,* not instructional activities. They do serve value in holding students accountable for completing their work and helping us—and the students—know if they understand the reading, but they don't *cause* students to understand.

It's important here to distinguish the difference between comprehension questions—questions designed to check students' understanding—and what I have come to call *strategic questions*, which are designed to help students penetrate complex texts. This chapter is actually designed to help you use these kinds of questions as a strategy to help you build strong readers. Strategic questions are thoughtfully designed to help students notice, reflect on, and form hypotheses about key aspects of complex texts. When well designed and well employed, strategic questions can actually cause students to understand versus simply measure what they understand. Most comprehension questions aren't strategically designed. We will dig more into designing strategic questions later in this chapter.

Shifting to Prepare-Process-Assess

In the strategizing phase of up-front planning, teachers think about both the texts they have chosen and the reading needs of the students they are teaching and try to make a match between the two. Mark hadn't really thought much about how to help his students actually read the texts he had collected. He and I talked about moving from the two-part "assign and assess" paradigm to a three-part paradigm that engages students more deeply with complex texts.

Prepare-Process-Assess		
Prepare	**Process**	**Assess**
Remind students of the context or the purpose for reading. Clarify the learning target. Help students build essential background knowledge if it can't be built from the text they are about to read. If there is vocabulary that students absolutely need to know to understand the text, ensure that they know it.	Students read once for the gist, noting what they understand and don't understand. This is "low stakes" reading. They are independently giving it a shot. Let them struggle a bit. Teacher and students discuss key vocabulary. Teacher and students revisit the text through strategic questions. Students work in small groups to complete tasks that help them further discuss and process the text. This work may be differentiated. Students make or do something to solidify their understanding.	Periodically check on students' acquisition of skills by asking them to read new complex texts and answer strategic questions on their own. Use all kinds of formative assessments, including studying students' annotations and listening in on their conversations, to think about what they are thinking about.

As I work with teachers, two parts of this chart rapidly become conversations. The first is the notion that students will read, on their own, a text that the teacher has deliberately chosen to be "hard." Many teachers rapidly grow concerned that their kids won't "get it," and they *always* bring up their most struggling readers as examples of students who will be particularly impacted by this approach. Remember the purpose of the first read. It's not for all kids to get it. It's for all kids to start to work on getting it, a very first step. It's also to start to build in our students the confidence that, through persistent work, they *can* make hard text make sense. In some settings, in some instances, for some kids, this very first read could be a well-delivered teacher read-aloud. Not a halting read-aloud by the kids, going up and down rows, but a fluent, well-inflected read-aloud that gives students access to the text.

The second part of the chart that often raises concern is the approach of just telling kids what certain vocabulary words mean. This is another decision based on purpose. When choosing a complex text, one of the factors you're likely to consider is vocabulary. Thoroughly pre-teaching all of the vocabulary in a particular text would take lots of precious time. That's not to say you should never teach vocabulary in more in-depth ways. In fact, learners need multiple encounters with new words before they store them in long-term memory. But not all words are equal; some you will mention just to give kids access to the text. Others you will explore more thoroughly because they are "high-value" and have applicability beyond the moment.

As we talked, Mark and I had another big "aha" about his planning process. One of the reasons he had never really worked on the "process" portion of the "prepare-process-assess" paradigm is because he almost always relegated reading to homework, something his students were expected to do independently. Although there is great value in kids reading outside of school, really helping students learn to tackle complex texts has to happen *with* the teacher, and often with peers as well. Reading has to fit into the time when teachers and kids are together, at least some of the time.

This was a huge push for Mark, as it is for many content-area teachers, particularly high school teachers. It's a huge leap of faith to change practices from a lecture format, which offers the security of having "covered" all of the necessary topics, to a constructivist format, in which teachers and kids work together to develop understanding of a topic or concept by reading, talking, organizing, drawing, and writing about it.

As Mark studied the Common Core Standards for Literacy in History/Social Studies, Science & Technical Subjects, he realized that his vision of his students as independent, critical thinkers could be realized if he taught his students the skills outlined by the Standards. Of course he wanted his student scientists to "cite evidence," to "summarize ideas," to make sense of integrated data and text, and to evaluate the claims and supporting evidence of other scientists. But his students were not going to develop those skills by listening to Mark's lectures and taking notes. He saw that he needed to shake up his teaching style a bit to make room for his students to practice reading scientific texts. We talked about how to make that fit and agreed that he could tighten things up enough to spend part of two to three class periods in the upcoming evolution unit to dig into a complex text together.

As Mark thought about teaching his students about evolution, it seemed natural, and even important, that the students actually read some of Darwin's *The Origin of Species*. In fact, he thought it would help his students better understand the content of the unit if they approached the study of evolution with an understanding of the impact of Darwin and his work. Mark intentionally added literacy standards to his Standards-Targets-Assessments planner, just like social studies teacher Rich Richardson did in Chapter 3.

Here's Mark's initial planner for the evolution unit, **prior to** thinking about how he could work with students and how students could work together, to process a complex text. Notice how he had a clear intention of teaching his students to read to evaluate Darwin's thinking, but he had not yet been able to name how he might assess if his students could do it. He also had a sense that digging into *The Origin of Species* would help his students think more critically about the theory of evolution, but he was not yet sure how to assess that either.

Mark's Standards-Targets-Assessments Planner Before Our Work Together

NEXT GENERATION SCIENCE STANDARD* LS3B: Variation of Traits

In sexual reproduction, chromosomes can sometimes swap sections during the process of meiosis (cell division), thereby creating new genetic combinations and thus more genetic variation. Although DNA replication is tightly regulated and remarkably accurate, errors do occur and result in mutations, which are also a source of genetic variation. Environmental factors can also cause mutations in genes, and viable mutations are inherited (HS-LS3-2).

Environmental factors also affect expression of traits, and hence affect the probability of occurrences of traits in a population. Thus the variation and distribution of traits observed depends on both genetic and environmental factors (HS-LS3-2) (HS-LS3-3).

Long-Term Targets	Supporting Targets	Assessments
I can analyze the processes that lead to changes in individual organisms and species over time.	I can explain the theory of evolution.	Notes "quick quiz" Peppered Moth Lab Final exam
	I can explain how new combinations of existing genes or mutations lead to changes in inheritable characteristics.	Quick quiz Chapter questions
	I can explain the process of natural selection and the concept of "survival of the fittest."	Chapter questions Beaks of Finches Lab Report Final exam
	I can analyze the evolutionary "tree" of various organisms.	Relationships and Biodiversity Lab
	I can explain why some species adapt to changed environmental conditions while others become extinct.	Chapter questions *?? Seems like something from* The Origin of Species *fits here*

continues

Long-Term Targets	Supporting Targets	Assessments
I can successfully conduct valid scientific investigations.	I can safely use all laboratory equipment.	Observation during lab periods
	I can formulate hypotheses.	Lab reports
	I can collect, organize, and analyze data.	Lab reports
	I can draw valid conclusions.	Lab reports
I can delineate and evaluate the argument and specific claims in *The Origin of Species,* including the validity of the reasoning, as well as the relevance and sufficiency of the evidence.	I can identify Darwin's claims and the evidence he uses to support them.	??
	I can summarize selections from *The Origin of Species.*	*?? Some kind of summary, but how do I get them there?*

*Next Generation Science Standards is a registered trademark of Achieve. Neither Achieve nor the lead states and partners that developed the Next Generation Science Standards was involved in the production of, and does not endorse, this product.

Foundational Strategies: Close Reading and Strategic Questioning

I wanted to help Mark address the question marks in his Standards-Targets-Assessments planner, so I started by teaching him about two important foundational strategies for helping students learn to read and understand complex text. All teachers hoping to help students become better readers of complex text need to know these foundational strategies. The first is close reading, a process through which students slowly and carefully make meaning of complex text by examining it from multiple angles. The second, related strategy, is strategic questioning, what some call "text-dependent questioning." I like the term *strategic questioning* because I have come to see this type of questioning as just that: a strategy that scaffolds students' understanding. When done well, strategic questioning can literally lift students up to a challenging text, enabling them to understand more about a text than if they are left on their own.

Close reading is a process that spans the "prepare-process-assess" paradigm of lessons designed around a complex text. Teachers must plan close-reading lessons carefully, as they are different from lessons in which students are reading simple, straightforward text. There are three goals in close-reading lessons. First, students learn about whatever they are reading about, the content, or story, the text contains. Second, students learn about vocabulary and syntax, and, with enough close reading, integrate new words and structures into their own writing and thinking. Third, they learn about the text itself—how it is written, the specific structures the author employed, the words the author chose, the impact the author was trying to make, and the strength of the author's argument. The second and third objectives of close-reading lessons are new ideas for many content-area teachers, and even some English/Language Arts teachers.

In close-reading lessons, the teacher is serving as the students' reading "guide." This means that the teachers themselves have already become experts on a particular text and are prepared to lead students down the trail of understanding while keeping them from getting lost through trail markers and signposts. The "trail markers" and "signposts" are the structures and strategic questions teachers use to help students navigate the text. Students have to travel the trail, the guide can't walk it for them, but the guide can also keep novice readers from ending up on the wrong mountain, or quitting because they are too exhausted to continue.

Preparing Students for Close Reading

The "prepare" portion of close-reading lessons is critical and subtly complicated. The trick is to prepare students just enough to get them started on the trail, but not to overly prepare them to the point that the hike—reading the text itself—is no longer necessary.

Mark was pretty sure he was preparing his students to read, and he was. But at first he was making a very common mistake, which was to tell his students too much about what they were getting reading to read. He said things like, "OK, we've been talking about Darwin and natural selection. Today we are going to read Darwin's actual writing on the topic. In this book that he wrote in 1859, called *On the Origin of Species by Means of Natural Selection*, Darwin said organisms of the same species have to compete for resources. Therefore, organisms that have advantages—that are faster, stronger, or have genetic variations, such as longer beaks or better camouflage—are more likely to survive and pass those characteristics on to their offspring. OK, let's see how Darwin explains it." Mark thought he was reassuring his students that they could handle the complex text that they were getting reading to dig into. But his kids were sitting there thinking, "Do I really need to read this? I think I might already know about this natural selection thing." I reminded Mark of the essential elements of preparing students to read complex text:

> Remind students of the context or purpose for reading.
> Clarify the learning target.
> Help students build essential background knowledge if it can't be built from the text they are about to read.
> If there is vocabulary that they absolutely need to know to understand the text, ensure that they know it.

The next period, Mark changed his introduction to the text like this:

"We've learned a bit about evolution, and today we're going to dig in a little further. We are continuing to work on our target 'I can explain the theory of evolution.' Christina, help us out with this word *theory*. Why is it a 'theory' of evolution? . . . Good, in science, a theory isn't just a guess. It's an explanation supported by reliable knowledge. One specific person—Charles Darwin—contributed a great deal to the theory of evolution by writing about what is called *natural selection*. We are going to read some of his writing today, from a book he wrote in 1859 called *The Origin of Species by Means of Natural Selection*. Who knows what the word *origin* means?"

A Close Look at Close Reading

For his first 20-minute reading lesson, Mark chose a small chunk of *The Origin of Species* to start with: the first paragraph of the introduction. He wanted his students to understand a bit about Darwin as a person and a scientist before they read his actual arguments. Here's the first text Mark asked his students to read:

> "When on board H.M.S. Beagle, as naturalist, I was much struck with certain facts in the distribution of the inhabitants of South America, and in the geological relations of the present to the past inhabitants of that continent. These facts seemed to me to throw some light on the origin of species—that mystery of mysteries, as it has been called by one of our greatest philosophers. On my return home, it occurred to me, in 1837, that something might perhaps be made out on this question by patiently accumulating and reflecting on all sorts of facts which could possibly have any bearing on it. After five years' work I allowed myself to speculate on the subject, and drew up some short notes; these I enlarged in 1844 into a sketch of the conclusions, which then seemed to me probable: from that period to the present day I have steadily pursued the same object. I hope that I may be excused for entering on these personal details, as I give them to show that I have not been hasty in coming to a decision."

Mark asked his students to read this short chunk of text silently, once all the way through, asking themselves, "What is this mostly about?" He also asked them to circle words or phrases they felt like they didn't really understand and needed to understand in order to really "get" the paragraph.

This first read of a complex text is intentionally broad; its purpose is simply to orient the readers to the text and to start to develop meaning. When Mark saw that most of his students were finished reading, he asked them to talk to each other about what they thought the text was mostly about. "Darwin is explaining his process," one student said. "He got an idea while he was on a trip and he's been thinking about it a long time," said another. Mark called on a few pairs to explain their thinking to the class and affirmed that they were on the right track.

"What words or sections are tripping you up?" Mark asked the class. "Geological relations," one student said while many others nodded. "'Mystery of mysteries?' Who said that?" another student wanted to know. "I don't get what he means by 'sketch of the conclusions,'" said a third.

Mark explained that the man Darwin called a "philosopher," who had described evolution as the "mystery of mysteries," was Sir John Herschel, whom Darwin had met while he was still a young man and whom he deeply respected and admired. There was no way for the students to figure that out from the text; it was background knowledge that simply had to be supplied or found in another source. But Mark wanted his students to see if they could figure out "geological relations" and "sketch of the conclusions."

"Listen to this sentence and see if you can make an inference about what 'sketch of the conclusions' is," he said. "'After five years' work I allowed myself to speculate on the subject, and drew up some *short notes*; these I *enlarged* in 1844 into a sketch of the conclusions, which then seemed to me probable.' Talk to each other. What might a 'sketch of the conclusions' be, based on what he says in the rest of the sentence?"

The students talked for just a minute, and then Mark asked the student who had offered "sketch of the conclusions" as a sticking point if he'd made any sense of it. "Well, he started with notes and then made it bigger," the student said. "I think it might be like his first draft? And once he wrote his first draft he started feeling like his ideas were right?"

"Right on," Mark said. "You just used context to make 'sketch of the conclusions' make sense. That's exactly what you should try when you don't understand something."

"OK, let's try 'geological relations,'" Mark prompted. "I think you're going to get this one by re-reading the text and also by thinking about what you already know about 'geological' and 'relations.' Talk to each other, and see if you can figure it out." They did.

"Great. Now that we have the basic meaning down, let's see what more we can figure out about Darwin from this short passage," Mark encouraged. He asked his first strategic question: "What kind of scientist was he? Read the passage again and underline specific details that give you an idea about the way he worked and thought."

The students did, underlining words and phrases like "struck with certain facts," "patiently accumulating," "reflecting," "five years' work," "allowed myself to speculate," "steadily pursued," "not been hasty."

"He was careful," the students concluded. "He worked really hard on this and didn't jump to conclusions." "It's like he was using the scientific process, only really slowly."

"Why would Darwin start his book this way?" Mark asked the students. "Why take the time to let readers know how long he had worked on this?"

"It's like he wanted people to know he had really studied his own idea," a student said. "Maybe he was afraid they wouldn't believe him?"

"You're right. Let's think about that," Mark said. "It was 1859. Evolution was a relatively new idea that many people didn't really know about. In fact, Darwin was criticized by many people in his time, and he knew he would be. He had to construct a rock-solid argument to get people to consider what he had to say. We're going to look at parts of his argument together tomorrow."

Mark and his students had tackled the basic structure of close-reading lessons. They had:

> › read the text once, for the gist, noting what they understood and didn't understand

> › discussed key vocabulary

> › revisited the text multiple times through strategic questions.

Mark had been careful to provide his students with only the information they needed to get started and to clarify only what they could not make sense of by re-reading and talking with each other. Mark's questions were strategic, which helped the students get to the understanding that Mark had intended. Over time, teachers asking students to read closely can expect that students will start to develop their own internal questions to help them understand an author's purpose. But, for now, Mark's students benefited from the scaffold that his strategic questions provided. Mark could have told them that Darwin was a good scientist, but that would have been virtually meaningless. He allowed them to discover that by examining Darwin's own writing.

Strategies That Help Students Dig Even Deeper

Mark's students were off to a good start, but they still hadn't hit the target Mark really wanted them to: analyzing Darwin's arguments related to natural selection. He also wanted to collect something from every student so he could have a look at each kid's thinking. Mark and his class were ready for the next part of the "process" phase of text-based lessons. They needed to:

> › Work in small groups to complete tasks that would help the students further discuss and process the text. (Potentially, this work is differentiated in purposeful and thoughtful ways, as described in Chapter 5.)

> › Make or do something to solidify their understanding.

Together, Mark and I looked at more of Darwin's writing and selected another chunk for the class to work on. Here's the paragraph we chose, from Chapter 3: The Struggle for Existence:

Climate plays an important part in determining the average numbers of a species, and periodical seasons of extreme cold or drought, I believe to be the most effective of all checks. I estimated that the winter of 1854–55 destroyed four-fifths of the birds in my own grounds; and this is a tremendous destruction, when we remember that ten per cent is an extraordinarily severe mortality from epidemics with man. The action of climate seems at first sight to be quite independent of the struggle for existence; but in so far as climate chiefly acts in reducing food, it brings on the most severe struggle between the individuals, whether of the same or of distinct species, which subsist on the same kind of food. Even when climate, for instance extreme cold, acts directly, it will be the least vigorous, or those which have got least food through the advancing winter, which will suffer most. When we travel from south to north, or from a damp region to a dry, we invariably see some species gradually getting rarer and rarer, and finally disappearing; and the change of climate being conspicuous, we are tempted to attribute the whole effect to its direct action. But this is a very false view: we forget that each species, even where it most abounds, is constantly suffering enormous destruction at some period of its life, from enemies or from competitors for the same place and food; and if these enemies or competitors be in the least degree favoured by any slight change of climate, they will increase in numbers, and, as each area is already fully stocked with inhabitants, the other species will decrease. When we travel southward and see a species decreasing in numbers, we may feel sure that the cause lies quite as much in other species being favoured, as in this one being hurt. So it is when we travel northward, but in a somewhat lesser degree, for the number of species of all kinds, and therefore of competitors, decreases northwards; hence in going northward, or in ascending a mountain, we far oftener meet with stunted forms, due to the *directly* injurious action of climate, than we do in proceeding southwards or in descending a mountain. When we reach the Arctic regions, or snow-capped summits, or absolute deserts, the struggle for life is almost exclusively with the elements.

Mark was aware that Darwin's writing—including this section of *The Origin of Species*—often followed a pattern of making a point, then supporting that point with a variety of evidence. This was the pattern he wanted his students to discover. I introduced Mark to a simple Claim-Evidence-Interpretation graphic organizer, which could be used both while reading, to examine the structure of an argument, and as a planning tool in preparation for writing an argument.

Claim-Evidence-Interpretation
Claim (the thesis, or argument):
Evidence (facts, data, and details that support the claim):
Interpretation (the "so what," or conclusion you draw from this section):

In his next close-reading lesson, Mark used the basic structure of close reading to introduce his students to the new section of *The Origin of Species*. They read it once, on their own, for gist, noting the vocabulary and syntactical challenges that kept them from understanding. (The sentence "Even when climate, for instance extreme cold, acts directly, it will be the least vigorous, or those which have got least food through the advancing winter, which will suffer most" was a heart-stopper in this section. The "it" seems to reference "extreme cold" rather than the "least vigorous." Darwin's editor must have missed that one!)

Then the students discussed their confusions, re-reading and talking together to figure out the passage. Mark used strategic questions, such as "In the first couple of sentences, what does Darwin say about the way climate impacts living organisms?" and "What is the 'false view?'" Mark asked the students to draw a box around the text, from the beginning up to "false view," and another box around the text after that sentence. "What do you notice?" he asked the class. "Talk together about the structure of this section."

"He first says what a lot of people might think, but then he corrects that idea," one pair offers. "Right, it's like he is showing that it's not so simple as whether or not there's enough food," adds another group.

Once the students had a basic understanding of Darwin's argument, Mark showed them a completed model of a Claim-Evidence-Interpretation graphic organizer, based on a different paragraph of *The Origin of Species* than the one they read. Here's the section of text he used for the model, also from Chapter 3: The Struggle for Existence:

> There is no exception to the rule that every organic being naturally increases at so high a rate, that if not destroyed, the earth would soon be covered by the progeny of a single pair. Even slow-breeding man has

doubled in twenty-five years, and at this rate, in a few thousand years, there would literally not be standing room for his progeny. Linnaeus has calculated that if an annual plant produced only two seeds and there is no plant so unproductive as this and their seedlings next year produced two, and so on, then in twenty years there would be a million plants. The elephant is reckoned to be the slowest breeder of all known animals, and I have taken some pains to estimate its probable minimum rate of natural increase: it will be under the mark to assume that it breeds when thirty years old, and goes on breeding till ninety years old, bringing forth three pairs of young in this interval; if this be so, at the end of the fifth century there would be alive fifteen million elephants, descended from the first pair.

And here's the model graphic organizer:

Claim (the thesis, or argument):
Organisms reproduce so often that if something didn't happen to destroy them, the earth would be overrun with living things.

Evidence (facts, data, and details that support the claim):
- The human population doubles every 25 years. If that kept up, there wouldn't be enough room for people to stand next to each other.
- If plants created only two seedlings a year, and if those two seedlings had two, and so on, it would result in a million plants.
- The descendants of two elephants could be as many as fifteen million.

Interpretation (the "so what," or conclusion you draw from this section):
Something must be happening that limits the amount of offspring that living things produce.

After showing students the graphic organizer, Mark then asked, "What do you notice about the evidence Darwin used to support his claim in this section?" "It's mathematical," a student replied. "He gives three specific examples and they all make the same point," said another.

Mark also showed students a rubric that he would use to assess their graphic organizers and asked students to apply the rubric to the model he had just shared.

Mark asked his students to gather in groups of three to complete the graphic organizer by identifying Darwin's claim, evidence, and interpretation in the section they had worked on that day. This lesson took about forty minutes, a whole-class period. He collected the graphic organizers to spot-check students' understanding and was pleased to see that all the students were able to identify the claim, evidence, and a collective interpretation, and they were mostly able to restate the section accurately in their own words.

Criteria	Exemplary	Does the Job	Not Yet
Identification of Claim and Evidence	Claim is completely identified. All of the evidence presented is included.	Claim is adequately identified, although some parts of the claim might be missing or confused. Most of the evidence, including the most important evidence, is included.	Claim isn't identified. Only some evidence is included, or lots of evidence is included but the most important evidence is missing.
Interpretation	Shows thorough and deep understanding of the passage.	Shows mostly accurate understanding of the passage.	Shows misunderstanding, or little or no understanding, of the passage.
Translation	Accurately translated using clear, sophisticated, scientific language.	Accurately translated, but sometimes falls back on kid language or weak language (stuff, things, etc.).	Inaccurately translated and/or an over-reliance on kid language ('cuz, etc.).

In his third close-reading lesson of the evolution unit, Mark introduced a third section from *The Origin of Species*. Students read for gist, noted confusions, and talked with each other and with Mark to clarify. Then he showed the class a few great graphic organizers from their previous work and asked them to complete the Claim-Evidence-Interpretation organizer on their own. He did work directly with one small group that was composed of kids who struggled when they had tried it together the first time. Once the students had completed the graphic organizer, Mark cold called on a few kids to share how they had restated certain portions of the text, and he reinforced the expectation that students try to use clear, scientific language. This also took a large portion of a class period, about thirty minutes. (Mark uses the "cold call" strategy often in his class. Cold calling involves giving kids think time and then randomly calling on students rather than asking who knows the answer or calling on students with their hands raised. This approach holds students accountable for reading).

Then Mark showed the students how he had written a summary from the graphic organizer he showed them as a model and asked them to write their own summaries as homework. Mark collected and carefully read the students' graphic organizers, scoring them using the rubric. He also looked at their summaries to see if students were translating their graphic organizers well. A few days later, he showed the students a few exemplary graphic organizers and paragraphs and allowed any students who wanted to rewrite theirs to try again.

Moving forward, Mark decided to use selections from *The Origin of Species* as "warm-ups" during some class periods. He also assigned another independent reading assignment with a relatively straightforward section of the text as a homework assignment. Finally, he decided to add a selection from *The Origin of Species*, along with strategic questions and a Claim-Evidence-Interpretation graphic organizer and rubric, to his final exam for the unit.

Assessing Students' Reading Work

Now Mark had the artifacts he needed to assess whether or not his students' had met both the content and literacy learning targets in his evolution unit. We went back to his Standards-Targets-Assessments planner and completed it, like so:

Mark's Standards-Targets-Assessments Planner After Our Work Together

NEXT GENERATION SCIENCE STANDARD LS3B: Variation of Traits

In sexual reproduction, chromosomes can sometimes swap sections during the process of meiosis (cell division), thereby creating new genetic combinations and thus more genetic variation. Although DNA replication is tightly regulated and remarkably accurate, errors do occur and result in mutations, which are also a source of genetic variation. Environmental factors can also cause mutations in genes, and viable mutations are inherited. (HS-LS3-2)

Environmental factors also affect expression of traits, and hence affect the probability of occurrences of traits in a population. Thus the variation and distribution of traits observed depends on both genetic and environmental factors (HS-LS3-2) (HS-LS3-3).

Long-Term Targets	Supporting Targets	Assessments
I can analyze the processes that lead to changes in individual organisms and species over time.	I can explain the theory of evolution.	Notes "quick quiz" Peppered Moth Lab Final exam
	I can explain how new combinations of existing genes or mutations lead to changes in inheritable characteristics.	Quick quiz Independent reading and answering strategic questions of one section of *The Origin of Species* (at home) Questions 1–2 from the textbook
	I can explain the process of natural selection and the concept of "survival of the fittest."	Questions 3–4 from the textbook Beaks of Finches Lab Report Reading, questions, and graphic organizer on unit exam
	I can analyze the evolutionary "tree" of various organisms.	Relationships and Biodiversity Lab
	I can explain why some species adapt to changed environmental conditions while others become extinct.	Chapter questions Summary from *The Origin of Species* (started in class)

continues

Long-Term Targets	Supporting Targets	Assessments
I can successfully conduct valid scientific investigations.	I can safely use all laboratory equipment.	Observation during lab periods
	I can formulate hypotheses.	Lab reports
	I can collect, organize, and analyze data.	Lab reports
	I can draw valid conclusions.	Lab reports
I can delineate and evaluate the argument and specific claims in *The Origin of Species,* including the validity of the reasoning, as well as the relevance and sufficiency of the evidence.	I can identify Darwin's claims and the evidence he uses to support them.	Claim-Evidence-Interpretation graphic organizers from class, homework, and final exam
I can comprehend selections from *The Origin of Species.*	I can identify the central idea of selections from *The Origin of Species.* I can summarize selections from *The Origin of Species.*	Claim-Evidence-Interpretation graphic organizers from class, homework, and unit exam Summary paragraph from unit exam

Mark learned through this experience that assessing his students' capacity to read complex text could happen only after he spent time helping them learn how to do it and developing a vision of what it meant to be successful doing it. Just like Rich, the social studies teacher in Chapter 3, Mark took steps to bring his students into the conversation about what it meant to be successful with the work he asked them to complete. He provided his students with models and exemplars; a clear, student-friendly rubric; and targeted feedback as they learned the process over time.

Designing Close-Reading Lessons

Designing close-reading lessons is not a recipe or a formula. It's a series of decisions based on the text to be taught, the targets a teacher is trying to help students reach, the students themselves, and the time available. What follows is a list of decisions I make when preparing lessons that involve close reading of complex texts:

1. First, I have to decide how well I know the text I am planning to teach. Often, I have to read the text closely myself. I read it once, for the gist, trying to get a sense of the "whole" of it. As I am reading, I think about the parts that come easily to me, and I underline the places where I am initially confused. Then I re-read those parts again, seeing if I can make them make sense.

2. Sometimes I decide I have to read *about* the text, as well. I learn more about its historical or cultural context, or more about the topic the text is conveying, or what critics have said about it. I might have to double-check specific word meanings. Then I read the text I intend to teach again, with those things in mind.

3. Once I feel as if I really understand the text myself, I think more about the learning target that I hope the text will help the students reach. Does this text really do the job? Do I need to adjust the target because I really want to use this text? Or do I look for another text that meets the target?

4. When I am sure there's a match between the text and the target, I think about how I will scaffold students to help them discover what they need from the text, while still leaving space and time for them to have their own revelations. I think about the vocabulary words that students might need support with, and I re-read the text to see if they could figure out those words in context.

5. I plan strategic questions that will point students in the right direction and both enable them to discover critical, explicit information and develop inferences they can support with evidence. (See the next section in this chapter, Designing Strategic Questions, for more information.)

6. Launching a close-reading lesson in the right way is critical, as we learned from Mark's example. Planning how to introduce the text—giving students just enough to get them started without squashing their need or desire to read—is an essential step.

7. I think about what I want students to do to capture their thinking, as a result of the reading. Do I want them to annotate their texts? Write on sticky notes? Talk to each other while I listen in? Complete some sort of notes or graphic organizer? I decide how much of the students' thinking I need to "see" during this lesson.

8. I decide whether or not the students need to go beyond the basic structure of close reading into small-group work that will help them look even more deeply into the text. If I do want them to go further, I consider the strategies I know that will provide some structure to that small-group work.

9. Finally, I decide what it will look like for the students to have been successful with this work. I create criteria or rubrics to share with students to help guide their work. I design or find models so I can coach them toward quality work.

Rest assured that, while this may seem daunting at first, the decisions that lead to well-designed close reading will become more "automatic" over time. For a while, it might be helpful to have a template to guide your decisions and coach you through the process. Here's one that many teachers have found helpful:

Close-Reading Lesson Planning Template
Learning Targets

Complex Text Being Read	Quantitative Factors	Qualitative Factors

Strategic Questions	Academic Vocabulary

Phase	Critical Moves	Your Plans
Prepare	Keep it short!	
Process	Work the text in chunks. Students read silently or the teacher might read aloud. Students mark text to indicate confusions. Teacher and students work together to resolve confusions. Students revisit text through strategic questions.	
	Students select evidence and formulate thoughts. Students organize thinking.	
	Partners and small groups work together to dig deeper.	
Assess	Check back on target. Assess students' process as well as understanding.	

This planning template is designed as a guide, not a rigid rule or protocol. Although this sequence seems clear on paper, your students are the variable. They may need to re-read the text several times before marking it, for example, or possibly the deeper digging happens after several cycles of reading, re-reading, and questioning. You know your students and your content best.

Designing Strategic Questions

Strategic questions, what many call *text-dependent questions*, are questions that, when fully answered, require students to return to the text, re-read, and select important details and key ideas from the text to formulate their responses. When designed and used well, strategic questions can also guide students through a complex text, prompting them to re-read and reconsider the words, phrases, and ideas. This will help them to not only understand the text but to also think about the author's purpose and to see the text within the broader context of texts both similar and different from it.

Strategic questions, which are both literal and inferential, generally fall into three broad categories.

1. Questions about what the text says, both explicitly and implicitly. These kinds of questions help students meet the College and Career Readiness Anchor Standards for Reading 1–3. When Mark asked his students "What kind of scientist was Darwin?" he was asking this kind of question.

   a. When reading fiction, these are questions about setting, plot, character, and theme.
   b. When reading expository text, these are questions about events, central and supporting ideas, and individuals.

2. Questions about the author's craft. These kinds of questions help students meet the College and Career Readiness Anchor Standards for Reading 4–6. When Mark had his students draw boxes around different sections of a text and then asked his students what they noticed about the structure of the paragraph, he was asking this kind of question.

   a. Regardless of whether reading fiction or expository texts, these are questions about word choice; language, structure, syntax, and grammar; and point of view and perspective.

3. Evaluation and analysis questions. These kinds of questions help students meet standards 7–9. When Mark asked his students "What do you notice about the evidence Darwin uses to support his claim?" he was asking this kind of question.

a. Regardless of whether reading fiction or expository texts, these are questions that ask readers to integrate information from various forms of text, to compare texts to other texts (including nontraditional texts), and to evaluate texts against a variety of criteria.

It's helpful, when starting to develop strategic questions, to have some starters to get you thinking about what to ask students to consider about a text. Whether selecting from this list or designing your own questions, remember to ask questions that will help your students meet the learning targets you've established for their reading.

Category of Question	Question Starter
Questions about what the text says, both explicitly and implicitly	*Who? What? Where? When? Why? Use specific details from the text to support your answer.* *Which details should be included in a summary of [BLANK]? Why?* *What conclusions can you draw about . . . ?* *What can you infer about . . . ?* *Why do you think that . . . ?"* *How could you explain . . . ?* *What reasons might explain . . . ?* *What does [BLANK] mean?* *What is the significance of . . . ?* *All of these kinds of questions should be followed by "What evidence can you draw from the text to support your answer?"*
Questions about the author's craft	*How would you define . . . ?* *In your own words, what is . . . ?* *Why did the author choose . . . ?* *Why does the author say . . . ?* *Where is an example of . . . ?* *How would this text be different if . . . ?* *How is (this section, paragraph) related to . . . ?* *Why did the author organize [BLANK]?* *What is the author's attitude toward . . . ? How do you know?* *What does the author want you to think about . . . ?* *What evidence do you have?*

continues

Category of Question	Question Starter
Evaluation and analysis questions	*How is [BLANK] like [BLANK]?*
	How is [BLANK] different from [BLANK]?
	What patterns can you find in . . .?
	How would you describe the organization of . . .?
	What is this author's argument? What evidence is used to support that argument?
	Which details does this author use to convince . . .?
	What, specifically, caused you to believe . . .?
	What, specifically, caused you to disagree . . .?
	What, specifically, makes this a good example of . . .?
	What, specifically, strengthens/weakens . . .?

When you start to use complex text and strategic questions with your students, start small. Ask questions that they can mostly likely answer. Give your students some early "wins" to build their confidence in making challenging text make sense. Before asking students to respond, give them time to talk with each other and write to collect their thoughts. Over time, students will start to internalize—and even mentally anticipate—the questions you might ask, especially if you use learning targets that help them understand how answering questions is helping them learn content and develop specific skills. At that point, they are ready to begin mentally questioning themselves to guide their own close reading—they will be that much closer to being "college and career" ready.

Selecting Additional Processing Strategies

Although close-reading lessons and strategic questions build students' comprehension of complex texts, there are many reasons to add additional processing strategies into the flow of lessons involving complex texts. For starters, as Mark learned, many common strategies will help teachers collect and examine artifacts of students' reading and thinking, for the purposes of both formative and summative assessment. In addition, many strategies provide a structure that will help students work together effectively. The addition of a processing strategy can help students dig even deeper into a text. And strategies like these keep the brainwork you are asking students to complete feel fresh and mentally stimulating.

The same way you want to ask questions that help your students meet a variety of learning targets aligned with a variety of standards, you want to select strategies that do the same. You'll find a bank of processing strategies at the end of this chapter, but first use this chart to help you identify the right strategies for your lessons.

College and Career Readiness Anchor Standards for Reading	Additional Strategies to Build This Skill
1. Read closely to determine what the text says explicitly and to make logical inferences from it; cite specific textual evidence when writing or speaking to support conclusions drawn from the text.	• Concept Ladder, p. 74 • Read Like a Reader/Read Like a Writer, p. 79 • Anticipation/Evidence Guides, p. 82 • Text-Tagging, p. 85 • Collaborative Comprehension, p. 92 • List-Group-Label, p. 102
2. Determine central ideas or themes of a text and analyze their development; summarize the key supporting details and ideas.	• Concept Map, p. 73 • Collaborative Comprehension, p. 92 • Summary Frame, p. 99, 100 • Summary Wheel, p. 99, 101
3. Analyze how and why individuals, events, and ideas develop and interact over the course of a text.	• Double Entry Journal, p. 77 • Collaborative Comprehension, p. 92
4. Interpret words and phrases as they are used in a text, including determining technical, connotative, and figurative meanings, and analyze how specific word choices shape meaning or tone.	• Concept/Vocabulary Sort, p. 76 • Read Like a Reader/Read Like a Writer, p. 79 • Contextual Redefinition, p. 103
5. Analyze the structure of texts, including how specific sentences, paragraphs, and larger portions of the text (e.g., a section, chapter, scene, or stanza) relate to each other and the whole.	• Read Like a Reader/Read Like a Writer, p. 79 • Preview and Predict, p. 84 • Claim-Evidence-Interpretation, p. 86 • Textbook Buddy, p. 88 • Jigsaw, p. 89
6. Assess how point of view or purpose shapes the content and style of a text.	• Double Entry Journals, p. 77 • Read Like a Reader/Read Like a Writer, p. 79 • It Says/I Say/And So, p. 90 • Collaborative Comprehension, p. 92 • Reading from Different Perspectives, p. 95
7. Integrate and evaluate content presented in diverse media and formats, including visually and quantitatively, as well as in words.	• Research Folders, p. 81 • Collaborative Comprehension, p. 92 • RAFT Reading and Writing, p. 97

continues

College and Career Readiness Anchor Standards for Reading	Additional Strategies to Build This Skill
8. Delineate and evaluate the argument and specific claims in a text, including the validity of the reasoning as well as the relevance and sufficiency of the evidence.	• Double Entry Journals, p. 77 • Anticipation/Evidence Guides, p. 82 • Claim-Evidence-Interpretation, p. 86 • It Says/I Say/And So, p. 90 • Reading from Different Perspectives, p. 95
9. Analyze how two or more texts address similar themes or topics in order to build knowledge or to compare the approaches the authors take.	• Research Folders, p. 81 • Anticipation/Evidence Guides, p. 82

Keys to Help You Make This Critical Move

To recap, helping students to meet the challenge of complex text involves planning and strategizing how to support students in actually reading the text, rather than merely assigning it. Teachers should develop a "prepare-process-assess" stance toward supporting students with reading complex text. Processing complex text includes:

> a basic close-reading structure

> strategic questions that help students notice key aspects of complex text

> additional processing strategies that help students dig deeper, often in small groups.

Works Cited

Allington, Richard. 2000. *What Really Matters for Struggling Readers*. Allyn & Bacon.

What They Are . . .

Concept Maps are graphic organizers that help students visualize various connections between words or phrases and a main idea. There are several types of Concept Maps; some are hierarchical, while others connect information without categorizing ideas.

Most Concept Maps consist of words or phrases surrounded by a circle or square and lines that connect to one another and, ultimately, back to the main idea. These lines help students make explicit their understanding of the relationship between details and main ideas.

Why They're So Great . . .

Concept Maps support struggling readers by building off of students' prior knowledge and asking them to reflect on their understanding while reading. Concept Maps are easy to construct and can be used across all content areas.

How to Create Them . . .

There are several ways to construct Concept Maps. Most include the following steps:

1. Model for your students how you think about what you already know and/or identify the main ideas presented in a text as you read.
2. Organize your ideas into categories, if applicable to the type of Concept Map you choose. Remind students that the organization may change as you continue to read and add more information.
3. Use lines or arrows to represent how ideas are connected to one another, a particular category, and/or the main idea.

How to Use Them . . .

- ▶ You can use Concept Maps as a pre-reading strategy by inviting students to share what they already know about a particular concept. As students begin reading and adding to the map, they are able to meld their prior knowledge with new information they gather from their reading.
- ▶ After students have finished, encourage them to share their Concept Maps with one another, in pairs or small groups. This will allow students to share and reflect on how they each interpreted the connections between concepts and words.
- ▶ After reading, ask students to revise their Concept Maps based on their new understandings.
- ▶ Encourage students to use Concept Maps to summarize what they have read, organize their writing on a concept, or to create a study guide for their own studying.

Works Cited

Hyerle, David. 1996. *Visual Tools for Constructing Knowledge*. Alexandria, VA: Association of Supervisors of Curriculum Development.

What It Is . . .

A Concept Ladder is an advance organizer that helps students develop questions to guide their close reading and understanding of a text. Students develop a question for each rung of the ladder based on their existing background knowledge, a class discussion, a photograph or gallery, or other experience. Then they read, looking for answers to their questions.

Why It's So Great . . .

When paired with intriguing pre-reading experiences or questions, Concept Ladders can be quite motivating to readers. Students are motivated to learn more, yet remain focused by their questions.

How to Use It . . .

First, carefully design a pre-reading experience that will engage students in thoughtful questioning. Then ask students to complete the Concept Ladder graphic organizer (see a sample on the next page). Students arrange their questions with the most "foundational" or basic at the bottom and the most "lofty" or higher-order at the top. They work to answer the questions from bottom to top. Students may share their questions with each other. Then students read the source material, looking for answers to their own questions.

For More Information . . .

Gillet, Jean, Charles Temple, and Alan Crawford. 2012. *Understanding Reading Problems: Assessment and Instruction*. Boston, MA: Little Brown.

Name _____ Date _____

Answer	Question

Answer	Question

Answer	Question

Answer	Question

Answer	Question

Answer	Question

What It Is . . .

Word Sorts involve categorizing words and/or ideas and/or parts of a topic. There are two types of Word Sorts: **closed** and **open**. In closed Word Sorts, the teacher defines the process for categorizing the words. This requires the students to engage in critical thinking as they examine vocabulary, corresponding concepts, or word structure. In open Word Sorts, the students determine how to categorize the words, thereby becoming involved in an active manipulation of words.

Why It's So Great . . .

It takes multiple encounters with vocabulary words before the words are deeply integrated into a learner's schema. Sorts are kinesthetic and feel a little like playing a card game. Kids tend to like this activity.

Sorts done with key words from the text *before* reading help students anticipate and build background about what's to come. Students' first attempts can be revisited after reading by asking them to move the words around or establish new categories, based on what they've learned.

How to Do It . . .

Sorts start with words on index cards or sticky notes. In a closed sort, the teacher tells the students which categories to use (e.g., "Put all the words that describe Holden in one pile and all the words that describe Huck Finn in another" "Put all the events of World War I in one pile and all those of World War II in another"). In an open sort, students examine all of the words and determine their own categories (e.g., "These words are about democracy, these are about communism, and these are about monarchies").

If done as a pre- and post-reading activity, have the students discuss their pre-reading sorts in pairs and then read for a short while, revisit the sort, read, revisit, etc.

For More Information and Other Options:

Visit: http://www.readwritethink.org/professional-development/strategy-guides/introducing-ideas-vocabulary-with-30953.html

What It Is . . .

A Double Entry Journal allows students to record their responses to text as they read. In the left-hand column or page, students copy or summarize text that they find to be intriguing, puzzling, or moving, or that connects to a previous entry or situation. In the right-hand column or page, students react to the quotation or summary. The entry may include a comment, a question, a connection made, or an analysis. Entries are made whenever a natural pause in the reading occurs so that the flow is not interrupted constantly.

Why It's So Great . . .

Double Entry Journals are open-ended and student-centered. They require students to figure out what's important and to respond to key points. They cause students to actually *think* rather than just skim for answers. Double Entry Journals foster the connection between reading and writing as students are able to "reply" to the author or speaker as they write their responses.

The technique offers flexibility in that teachers can use any form of written text, read-alouds, or other listening activities that are assigned in class.

How to Do It…

Left-Hand Side	Right-Hand Side
Quotes from the text (you might start this strategy with the teacher providing some quotes in this column, with space for students to add more).	Visual commentary (drawings, visual analogies, doodles)
Quotes from the text	Written reactions, reflections, commentary, musings ("Hmmm…")
Observations, details revealed by close reading	Significance
What the text says…	Why the text says this…
Questions: "I wonder why…"	Possible answers: "Maybe because…"
Quotes from texts	Questions (Clarifying & Probing)
Quotes from texts	Social Questions (Race, class, gender inequalities)
Quotes from texts	Memories
Quotes from texts	Naming Literary or Persuasive (Rhetorical) Techniques

What It Is . . .

This engaging strategy is ideal for helping students to slow down and read a text multiple times. The key is to help students sort out the thinking they do when they are reading like a *reader*—focused on the ideas and meaning of the text (the learning, connections, responses, and feelings the text evokes in them), and the thinking they do when they are reading like a *writer*—focused on the word choice, structure, techniques, and perspective of the author. Reading like a reader focuses the mind on the *what*: the content of the text. Reading like a writer focuses the mind on the *how*: the author's craft.

Why It's So Great . . .

This strategy requires readers to deliberately slow down and re-read with purpose. It is particularly powerful in helping readers step back from the meaning of the text to examine how the text was created. This is definitely a skill many students will benefit from developing.

How to Create It . . .

This strategy can be employed by simply asking students to think about the text's meaning on at least one pass of reading and the craft on another. However, most students benefit from a visual cue that helps them sort out their thinking. One way to do this is to have them read like a reader and jot notes in the margins in one color, and then use a different-colored pen or marker to write what they notice when reading like a writer. Another option is to create a graphic organizer like the one that follows. The text students will read goes in the center. What they notice about meaning goes on one side, and what they notice about craft goes on the other.

Read Like a Reader	Text	Read Like a Writer

For More Information:

Visit: www.ttms.org (Teaching That Makes Sense), a website by Steve Peha.

"Read Like a Reader, Write Like a Writer: A Powerful Approach to Reading Response" document available
   for download at www.ttms.org.

Read Like a Reader	Text	Read Like a Writer

What They Are . . .

A Research Folder is essentially a teacher-created, and therefore very managed and focused, Google search. A variety of readings, graphs, quotes, pictures, cartoons, etc., that are all related to a central topic, theme, or concept, are put in a folder. The folder is "browsed" by a small group of students or spread out around the room for all students to look at (this gets students out of their seats, which can be a very good thing!). A Research Folder is meant to be used at the beginning of a chunk of learning to build background and to get students interested in something they're going to learn more about.

Why They're So Great . . .

Research Folders enable teachers to invisibly differentiate texts, as each student selects the things he or she wants to look at or can make sense of. Students engage in silent reading about something they've chosen, most likely at a level that they can manage. All students then contribute to a group discussion or a shared task.

How to Create Them . . .

Gather resources, paying attention to finding information *in a variety of formats*. This takes some time, so think about setting up Research Folders with colleagues (e.g., "I'll do the roots of the Civil War if you do the Founding documents . . .") and then sharing them with each other. You might laminate the items in the folder so they can be used over and over. Provide a focus or task so the students know what they're browsing for.

How to Use Them . . .

Set and review a purpose for browsing. It's a good idea to have students browse silently for ten minutes or so, and then let them talk or write about what they are learning, then go back to silent browsing for another five minutes, and then talk or write again.

What It Is . . .

An Anticipation and Evidence Guide is a great pre-reading strategy that, when carefully structured, can provide a purpose for reading that helps students focus and gather the "right" details. It can also help them support their opinions about a text with evidence.

How It Helps Readers . . .

Anticipation Guides can be structured in many ways, but the template that follows helps readers confront their misconceptions or support their opinions with evidence. Previewing helps students build and activate background knowledge, preparing them for what they are about to learn. An interesting preview can motivate students to want to learn more.

How to Use It . . .

This strategy is particularly powerful when students are reading or discussing something they have misconceptions about, lack experience with, or are likely to have strong opinions about. Prior to reading, introduce an Anticipation Guide to students and have them agree or disagree with the center statements. If you like, have them discuss their opinions prior to reading. Then they read the selection. After reading, they must agree or disagree again, this time providing specific evidence from the text to "prove" their post-reading opinion is correct.

For More Information:

Rozzelle, Jan, and Carol Scearce. 2009. *Power Tools for Adolescent Literacy*. Bloomington, IN: Solution Tree Press.

Name _____ Date _____

Before Reading	Statement	After Reading
___ T ___ F		___ T ___ F

Evidence from text that supports your conclusion:

Before Reading	Statement	After Reading
___ T ___ F		___ T ___ F

Evidence from text that supports your conclusion:

What It Is . . .

Preview and Predict is a great strategy for getting students to notice all the good stuff in their textbooks and other expository texts that they usually skip over (the charts, maps, graphics, pictures, headings, bold words, etc.). Using this strategy, students spend a good chunk of time skimming a section of a textbook or text (starting with just a couple of pages), looking at everything *except* the writing. Students then write a prediction about what it is they are about to read. An enhancement is to have students write questions that they think will be answered in the text.

Why It's So Great . . .

Previewing helps students build and activate background knowledge, preparing them for what they are about to learn. It also builds students' awareness of the structure of texts. An interesting preview can motivate students to want to learn more.

How to Use It . . .

Introduce Preview and Predict with the most interesting material you can find. Challenge students *not* to read the text. Let them share their predictions with each other and discuss what they already know before diving into the text. If you are having them write questions, let students share their best questions and list them on the board. Ultimately, you want them to use Preview and Predict independently, to prepare for and engage in silent reading.

Be sure that the next phase in the reading takes students much more deeply into the information. You don't want Preview and Predict to take the place of actually reading the text.

For More Information:

Robb, Laura. 2003. *Teaching Reading in Social Studies, Science, and Math.* New York, NY: Scholastic Inc.

What It Is . . .

We often read aloud to students because we want to make sure they're paying attention and/or actually hearing the information we want them to understand. But listening is often passive, and it's very hard for teachers to know who's actually thinking about the reading and who's simply in outer space. Text-Tagging is marking, or annotating, the text. It provides students with a means to monitor their own thinking while reading, along with a "running record" of what's going on in their heads, which teachers can then examine for engagement and reflection. Adult readers text-tag all the time—remember your college textbooks?

Why It's So Great . . .

Text-Tagging helps improve comprehension on three fronts. First of all, students must read closely in order to create the tags. Second, they must pay attention to their own thinking as they work. Finally, the tags provide a kind of "running record" of their thinking, which enables them to share or build off of that thinking later on.

Text-Tagging is one piece of a reading strategy, but be sure students do more than "report" their own questions and connections. Combine with strategic questioning to ensure that students are returning to the text for a purpose. For example, Text-Tagging might be a great first step in preparing for a Socratic Seminar.

How to Create It . . .

Text-Tagging can either be teacher- or student-generated. You might start the process by requiring students to use the same symbols; for example, "?" for questions they have, "!" for new or interesting information, "*" for ideas or events that are important to remember, "_____" for key words, etc. Later on, proficient text-taggers might make the case for their own symbols.

How to Use It . . .

In order to tag the text, students will need either copies of the text to be read or sticky notes. Model Text-Tagging by reading and thinking aloud to the students; let them see you think about the text and use tags to record your thinking. Then have students read and tag short sections of text. Let them share with each other what they have marked and why. Collect and review tagged texts. Over time, students will build up to longer and longer reading and tagging sessions.

For More Information:

Harvey, Stephanie, and Anne Goudivs. 2007. *Strategies That Work,* Second Edition. Portland, ME: Stenhouse Publishers.

What It Is . . .

CEI is a graphic organizer that helps readers gather appropriate evidence and helps writers to organize paragraphs that incorporate evidence. Students work from a teacher-provided claim or develop their own "claim"—a statement that they are asked to, or want to, support with evidence. Then students gather and list evidence that supports their claim. Finally, students develop the interpretation, the "so what" of the paragraph. Ideally, you want to get to the point where students can read, develop a claim, and then re-read to support their claim.

How It Helps Readers . . .

Providing students with a claim can focus their reading on gathering evidence from a reading or a series of readings. This strategy also supports the writing of effective arguments.

How to Use It . . .

Start by having students read paragraphs written in the CEI format. Analyze the arguments and help students see that effective arguments have a logical flow.

Then you might transition into providing a claim and asking students to read source materials to determine what evidence makes the claim "true." Later on, support students in developing their own claims, or purposes for reading. Claims can have to do with anything—characters' motivations (e.g., Odysseus is physically strong), historical events, scientific principles, etc.

An example of this strategy in action, for both reading and writing, is found earlier in this chapter.

Name _____ Date _____

Claim (what you're trying to prove, your thesis, your argument):

Evidence (facts, data, and details that support your claim):

Interpretation (your "so what," your conclusion about the evidence):

What It Is . . .

Guided reading is a small-group teaching strategy that elementary teachers use to help students understand text that is just slightly above their reading level. During guided reading, teachers often "debug" the text and think aloud about how they handle tricky parts of text. They also point out to students the important things they're supposed to notice while reading. Textbook Buddies provide a scaffold for students who struggle to read textbooks (and which students don't?). It's kind of like a study guide, but instead of only providing questions for students to answer, the Textbook Buddy does what elementary teachers do—points out key features (e.g., "Did you notice the photograph on page 105? Take a few minutes to look it over, then write here about why it's important"), important ideas (e.g., "Notice the paragraph in the left-hand column about photosynthesis. Write the definition below, it's REALLY important"), and possible pitfalls (e.g., "I know, when I read that section about photosynthesis, I was confused too! Take a moment to write about what you THINK happens, and we'll talk more about this in class tomorrow").

How It Helps Readers . . .

Textbook Buddy reminds students to be metacognitive while reading. It also helps students to read independently, while still providing the guidance that less successful readers might need in order to learn content.

Why It's So Great . . .

The downside to study guides or comprehension questions is that students don't really read; they just skim for answers or copy off of each other at lunch! Textbook Buddies can help with that. Students will most likely still skip or skim the sections that the Textbook Buddy doesn't require them to read, but they will most likely get more out of the sections they *do* read. By writing in a conversational style, you can help make textbook study a little more interesting and "human." Plus, you can get your opinion in there!

How to Use It . . .

Truthfully, this is a lot of work for the teacher. For starters, you have to read the sections of the textbook you are assigning. You have to think about what your kids need to know, what they might miss, and what problems the textbook presents. On the other hand, this is your opportunity to be the "voice in the head" of students who are mindlessly scanning text or who are certain they just don't "get it." It makes sense to try Textbook Buddies with a couple of colleagues (e.g., "I'll write one for Chapter 2, you do Chapter 3, you do Chapter 4" etc.).

For More Information:

Daniels, Harvey, and Steven Zemelman. 2004. *Subjects Matter: Every Teacher's Guide to Content-Area Reading.* Portsmouth, NH: Heinemann.

What It Is . . .

The Jigsaw strategy can be a powerful cooperative-learning approach. A well-designed Jigsaw is like a jigsaw puzzle, in that "pieces" of study topics are researched by students within groups and then put together in the form of peer teaching between groups.

Students work in groups of three to six to become "experts" in one part of a topic of an overall theme or unit of study. The group members are charged with learning everything they can about their assigned topic. Their work should be checked before the next phase. In other words, give the experts a quiz or ask them to turn in writing or other products to be sure they are ready for the responsibility of the next phase.

Then the experts regroup so there is one of each kind of expert in the new groups. Experts teach each other what they have learned, and then the new group must DO something with the collective information. Note: The Jigsaw strategy works best when there is a product or an outcome required that *cannot be done without the expertise of each member of the group.*

Why It's So Great . . .

When the Jigsaw strategy is done well, students work collaboratively to solve a problem or to create a product that's somewhat bigger or meatier than any one student could do alone.

How to Do It . . .

1. Divide the class into 3–4 member groups (my experience is that 3 is the ideal number). Each member becomes an expert on a different topic/concept (experiment with choice—choice is motivating!).

2. Members of each team that has the same topic meet together in an expert group with a variety of resource materials and texts available to explore their topic.

3. The students work together to learn the information they are responsible for. It helps to have the expert groups complete a product or visual aid that they will use to teach the others. Check on the expertise of the "experts" before they go on to the next step.

4. Everyone returns to their original Jigsaw teams to teach what they learned to the other group members.

5. Team members listen and take notes as their classmate teaches them.

6. THIS IS THE MOST IMPORTANT STEP: The groups then use all of the information they have to make or do something. Allow them to use their notes or other resources from step five. This builds the "positive interdependence" that good cooperative learning requires.

For More Information:

Kagan, Spencer. 2009. *Kagan Cooperative Learning,* Second Edition. San Clemente, CA: Kagan Publishing.

What It Is . . .

It Says/I Say/And So is a graphic organizer that supports students in thinking about text at multiple levels. They select portions of text that they want to discuss with another student or in a small group. Then students read, either to answer a question or to find a section of text that intrigues them. They copy the text into the "It Says" box. Then they write their initial responses to the text in the "I Say" column. Students share their "It Says" and "I Say" with each other, taking the time to deepen their understanding and clarify. Finally, each student returns to their own graphic organizer to write the "And So," which is their synthesized understanding or reaction.

Why It's So Great . . .

This strategy can be used with teacher questions (see the example on the next page), with learning targets, or, very much like Double Entry Journals, this strategy enables students to choose the parts of a text that are important to them and respond in an open-ended way. In addition, this strategy prepares kids to talk with each other about what they've read.

How to Do It . . .

Create a chart or graphic organizer like the one that follows. Model for students your reading and thinking, and have them practice this initially with text they already understand. You are pushing kids toward higher-order thinking with this strategy, so be patient.

This strategy has the potential to help kids think more deeply about primary sources and to infer when reading literature.

For More Information:

Daniels, Harvey, and Steven Zemelman. 2004. *Subjects Matter: Every Teacher's Guide to Content-Area Reading.* Portsmouth, NH: Heinemann.

Name _____ Date _____ Text Title _____

Purpose for reading:

It Says	I Say	And So
(Select key ideas from the text that support your purpose for reading.)	(What's your interpretation, connection, response, or question related to this selection from the text?)	(So what? Why is this important? How does this information/idea support your task?)

What It Is . . .

In Collaborative Comprehension, students work in small groups to examine a text from multiple stances or angles. The stances are determined by the type of text it is and by the multiple ways a sophisticated reader would consider it. If it's literature, the stances are based on aspects of literature—characters, literary elements, word choice, plot elements, etc. If it's a primary source, the stances are historical accuracy, etc. (See the example role cards/prompts on the next page.) Each student takes on a certain stance and reads with the intention of helping the rest of the group understand the text from that stance.

Why It's So Great . . .

By working together and analyzing text in multiple ways, students develop a much deeper comprehension than they would alone. Even though they are reading the same text, each student is contributing something unique to the conversation. Furthermore, the stances can be thoughtfully assigned to students based on their difficulty—some stances are more concrete and therefore simpler than others.

How to Do It . . .

Start by finding or designing reading stances that work in your content area (some suggestions follow). Introduce each stance to your students separately and have them practice each one. This will give you the chance to see which stances work for which kids. Strategically place kids in groups so there's a good match for each stance in the group. Have them read and prepare, based on their stance. Students then share their thinking with the group. Undoubtedly, you will need to have some kind of accountability for the conversation, such as a discussion rubric.

Over time, you will want to wean your students off of reading and preparing for their single stance, only because proficient readers can think from multiple angles. After some practice with the stances, ask students to read more holistically and prepare for general discussion. Then, when students get to class, have them "draw" a stance, as if drawing from a pack of cards. This is now a discussion role vs. a reading stance. Give students ten minutes or so to re-read the source material and prepare for discussion, keeping in mind that they can also bring up and discuss anything they found in the reading that is outside of the role they drew. Moving the reading stances into discussion roles is an important next step.

For More Information:

This strategy is based on Literature Circles as initially described by Harvey Daniels in *Literature Circles: Voice and Choice in the Student-Centered Classroom*. Stenhouse Publishers, 1994.

Historian

Your task is to determine the historical context for the document/artifact. In order to accomplish this task, develop answers to the following questions:

- ► What is the artifact's date of origin?
- ► What do you already know about that time period?
- ► What do you know about the concerns and issues of someone from that time period?
- ► What do you see in the artifact that confirms or denies what you expected?

Authenticator

Your task is to determine whether or not the document/artifact is genuine. In order to accomplish this task, develop answers to the following questions:

- ► Who is the author/creator?
- ► Is it likely that the author/creator had firsthand knowledge of the events/issues depicted?
- ► Is the creator's point of view credible? Why or why not?

Impact Analyzer

Your task is to determine whether or not the document/artifact serves its intended purpose. In order to accomplish this task, examine the document/artifact and read it through at least once. Then develop answers to the following questions:

- ► What type of document/artifact is it? How was it developed/created?
- ► Who is the intended audience?
- ► Why was it developed in the form that it was?
- ► Was the artifact/document delivered to its intended audience? Can you tell how?
- ► Imagine that you are the person who first received/viewed this item. How does it make you feel? Why?

Content Master

Your task is to determine the "gist"—the main topic(s), or themes, of the document/artifact. In order to accomplish this task, read the document twice, once quickly and once slowly. After reading it quickly, write a list of ten key words and phrases from the document.

- ► Then complete the following statement: "This says that _____."
- ► Read it again to test your statement. Are you right? What would you change/add?

Collaborative Comprehension Roles for Science Reading

- ▸ The **Summarizer** summarizes the main idea of the article.
- ▸ The **Connector** makes connections between the text and other scientific principles.
- ▸ The **Investigator** looks up background material related to the article and helps fill in the background knowledge.
- ▸ The **Vocabulary Master** looks up and provides an understandable definition for vocabulary words that are unfamiliar or new.

Collaborative Comprehension Roles for Reading Literature

- ▸ The **Discussion Director** develops "meaty" questions for the group to discuss.
- ▸ The **Characterization Captain** tracks the development of characters.
- ▸ The **Literary Luminary** notes and describes the author's use of literary devices.
- ▸ The **Plot Master** charts rising action, the climax, and falling action on a chart for all group members to review.

There are no fixed rules here for these roles; do what you and your students need.

What It Is . . .

Reading from Different Perspectives is much like Collaborative Comprehension, except that rather than focusing on different aspects of the text, the students are thinking about how different readers would respond to or think about a text, or how different characters might see a particular incident. For example, while reading about genetics, students could wonder about how a scientist, a government official, a parent, and a not-yet-born baby would think about cloning. Students reading *To Kill a Mockingbird* could think not only about Scout's point of view as she watches the trial of Tom Robinson, which is right in the text, but could also infer how Boo Radley or Mrs. Dubose would be feeling and thinking if they were there. Students each complete one section of a graphic organizer while reading (see the graphic organizer on the following page) and then share their perspectives with each other. Reading from Different Perspectives is great when paired with RAFT writing (see page 97).

Why It's So Great . . .

Reading from Different Perspectives helps students develop critical thinking skills as they consider a text from multiple points of view. It challenges students not only to think about their own thinking but to think about the thinking of others who are different from themselves.

How to Do It . . .

Reading from Different Perspectives is easy to set up but more challenging to implement. Students will need models and examples in order to do this well. Start by asking students to think about a concept or question from two angles, then three, then four. This strategy works only when the text or issue being considered is worthy of a deeper look—it doesn't work with textbooks or single-aspect topics.

See the graphic organizer on the following page.

For More Information:

Based on "Thinking from Different Perspectives," p. 122, Billmeyer, Rachel. 2003. *Strategies to Engage the Mind of the Learner*. Rachel & Associates.

Topic or Question to be Considered

Perspective #1	Perspective #2

Perspective #3	Perspective #4

What It Is . . .

RAFT is an approach that asks students to read and write in order to learn (Mitchell 1996). Students learn to respond to a writing prompt that requires them to think about various perspectives, so it's a terrific follow-up to Reading from Different Perspectives (see previous entry).

When teachers develop a RAFT prompt, they consider the following:

- **R**ole of the Writer: Who are you as the writer? A pilgrim? A soldier? The President?
- **A**udience: To whom are you writing? A political rally? A potential employer?
- **F**ormat: In what format are you writing? A letter? An advertisement? A speech?
- **T**opic: What are you writing about?

How It Helps Readers . . .

RAFT helps readers make connections, ask questions, visualize, infer, determine importance, and synthesize. Students must think creatively and critically in order to respond to the prompt, making RAFT a unique way for students to apply critical-thinking skills about new information they are learning. RAFT writing is applicable in every content area, thereby providing a universal writing approach for content-area teachers.

How to Create It . . .

1. Explain to your students the various perspectives (mentioned above) that writers must consider when completing any writing assignment.

2. Display a RAFT writing prompt for your students, and model on an overhead or use a document camera to show how you would write in response to the prompt.

3. Use the RAFT reading organizer (see next page) to help students focus their reading on the key information they will need in order to complete their writing.

4. As students become comfortable reacting to RAFT prompts, you can create more than one prompt for students to respond to after a reading, lesson, or unit. Varied prompts allow students to compare and contrast multiple perspectives, deepening their understanding of the content.

Works Cited

Mitchell, Diana. 1996. "Writing to Learn Across the Curriculum and the English Teacher." *English Journal* 85: 93–97.

Santa, Carol M., Lynn T. Havens, and Bonnie J. Valdes. 2004. *Project CRISS: Creating Independence Through Student-owned Strategies,* Third Edition. Dubuque, IA: Kendall Hunt Publishing Company.

Element of RAFT	Specifics to Remember
ROLE *(What voice will I use in my writing? How will that impact my reading/info/data gathering?)*	
AUDIENCE *(Who am I communicating with? How will that impact my reading/info/data gathering?)*	
FORMAT *(What form will my message take? How does that impact my reading/info/data gathering?)*	
TOPIC *(What am I writing about? Use the space to the right to gather specific details that will be helpful.)*	

What It Is . . .

Summarizing is very complex but it shows us when students really deeply understand information from reading. I often ask adults in workshops to summarize their thinking, and often they do not—instead they "retell" a few points from the reading. When we effectively summarize, we take larger selections of text and reduce them to their bare essentials: the gist, the key ideas, the main points that are worth noting and remembering. It takes a bit of work to develop a summary that actually reflects the "whole" of a text.

How It Helps Readers . . .

Asking students to summarize is asking them to deeply consider the meaning of a text by distilling the message down to one or several main ideas or themes.

How to Do It . . .

Please be warned: teaching summarizing is no small undertaking. It's one of the hardest strategies for students to grasp and one of the hardest strategies for you to teach. You have to repeatedly model it and give your students ample time and opportunities to practice it. Can you imagine your students succeeding in school without being able to break down content into manageable, small, succinct pieces? We ask students to summarize all the time, but we're terrible about teaching them good ways to do this!

You might start with a Summary Frame graphic organizer (see page 100). Giving students these frames to complete after reading, processing, and discussing text helps them develop a "flow" for a summary. Don't hand out the Summary Frame and ask students to read to fill them in—that's a whole different mindset from summarizing. Instead, hold onto the frames until you have a sense that students are starting to understand the key ideas of a text.

Another helpful scaffold is the Summary Wheel or Summary Pizza (see page 101). You might start by putting the main ideas of a reading selection in the "crusts," and then asking students to add important details in the "slices." Then ask students to write several summary sentences; one for each slice. Later on, ask students to read the whole text, decide what idea should be in each crust, and then re-read for important details for each slice. Again, they should write a sentence for each.

For More Information:

Billmeyer, Rachel. 2003. *Strategies to Engage the Mind of the Learner.* Rachel & Associates.

Today's reading was about _____

_____

_____

_____

_____. One main idea was _____

_____

_____

_____

_____. This is important because _____

_____

_____

_____

_____. Another key idea is_____

_____

_____

_____.

This matters because_____

_____

_____

_____

_____. In summary, today's reading taught me _____

_____

_____

_____

_____

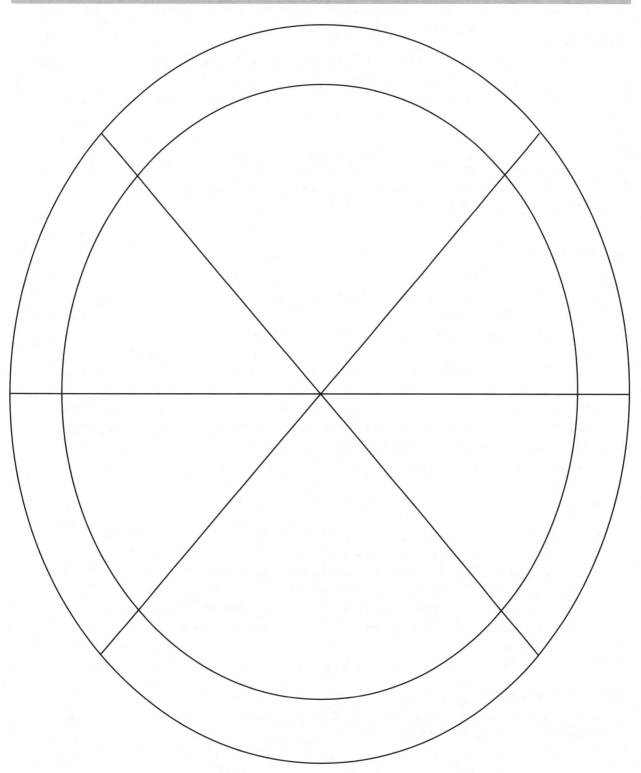

What It Is . . .

List-Group-Label is a vocabulary and/or pre- and post-reading strategy that engages students in a three-step process to build, activate, and organize their understanding of content-area vocabulary and concepts. Students literally create lists of words, group them, and label them prior to reading and then revisit their lists after reading.

Why It's So Great . . .

List-Group-Label makes words come alive for students through their conversations and reflections on the "meaning connections" between words. It actively engages students in learning new vocabulary and content and gets them interacting and debating.

How to Create It . . .

1. Select a main concept in a reading selection.
2. **List**: Have students brainstorm all the words or ideas they think relate to the topic they are getting ready to read about.
   a. Visually display student responses on the SMARTBoard, whiteboard, or on sticky notes.
   b. Do not critique students' responses; no answer is wrong at this point. Some words may not relate to the concept at hand, but hopefully students will realize this as they begin grouping the words in the next step.
3. **Group**: Divide your class into small groups. Each group will work to cluster the class list of words into subcategories that they determine. As groups of words emerge, challenge your students to explain their reasoning for placing words together or for discarding them.
4. **Label**: Ask the kids to develop a label or "title" for the groups of words they have developed.

How to Use It . . .

► Although List-Group-Label may begin as a pre-reading activity, students should return to it as they read through the text related to the major concept they brainstormed. They may find that they should add words from their reading or re-label the groups of words they created.

► Often, the best conversation between students centers around words that don't immediately fall into a major category at the beginning of the activity. Have students set those words aside in a "Huh?" box. As they read, students should determine if that word actually fits somewhere or if it is a misconception.

For More Information

Lenski, Susan D., Mary Ann Wham, and Jerry L. Johns. 1999. *Reading and Learning Strategies for Middle and High School Students*. Dubuque, IA: Kendall Hunt.

What It Is . . .

Contextual Redefinition offers students specific steps for deducing the meaning of unknown (or unclear) words in a reading passage by seeking clues from their context in a larger text selection.

Why It's So Great . . .

Contextual Redefinition helps students read closely to pay close attention to context, word order, syntax, and examples as they read. It helps deepen their word knowledge and explore multiple meanings of words. Students who use Contextual Redefinition often will develop a pattern of thinking about word meanings, "do I *really* know this word? How is it being used in *this* context?"

How to Use It . . .

1. Select several key words from a reading selection (look for words that have multiple meanings or that might otherwise be unclear to students). Write these words on the board.
2. Have students suggest definitions for these terms before reading the selection. Most likely, students will provide a range of definitions since the words are considered in isolation, without any specific context. Some of the proposed definitions will be inexact—hinting at, but not fully defining, the term.
3. Record all suggested definitions on the board.
4. Have students read the text selection, noting the specific sentences in which each of the words appears.
5. Ask students to revisit their previous definitions and see which, if any, reflect the use of these words in the context of the selection. Use dictionaries if student definitions lack enough clarity to match the contextual meaning of the words.
6. Reiterate that words have multiple meanings and uses and that the context of a word in a text selection determines its meaning.

For More Information

Lenski, Susan D., Mary Ann Wham, and Jerry L. Johns. 1999. *Reading and Learning Strategies for Middle and High School Students*. Dubuque, IA: Kendall Hunt.

Name _____

Date _____

DIRECTIONS:

▶ Look at the words in the first column.

▶ In the second column, rate each either 0 (no idea), 1 (I heard it but can't use it), or 2 (I can use it).

▶ In the third column, write what you think the word means before you read.

▶ Read the selection.

▶ In the fourth column, place a check if your definition remains the same.

▶ If your definition has changed, write your revised definition.

▶ In the last column, list any context clues that helped you more deeply understand the word.

1. Words	2. Prior Knowledge 0-1-2	3. Pre-Reading	4. Post-Reading	5. Clues

CHAPTER FIVE

PURPOSEFULLY DIFFERENTIATE

I became a teacher during a period of time when the inclusion of special education students in the general education setting was increasing significantly. My co-teacher, Judy, and I experienced the challenges and joys of teaching ninth-grade English to just about the most heterogeneous group of kids you can imagine. In one class we had a student with Asperger's syndrome, another with multiple sclerosis and blindness, two students with intellectual disabilities, some with learning disabilities, some with attention deficit disorder, some gifted kids, and a passel of "regular" kids—whoever they are.

It was great.

We had a blast co-teaching these classes. Judy and I balanced each other's strengths—where I was creative and a little flighty, she was organized. When I was moving fast, she was patient. When I was too forgiving, she was strict. We enjoyed the kids, and we enjoyed each other. It was a very popular class.

Judy and I thought we "differentiated" just about every lesson in one way or another. I put *differentiated* in quotes, because frankly, we deeply misunderstood how to differentiate well. It wasn't from a lack of care for the students—like many teachers, we intuitively understood that our students were really different from each other and therefore needed different ways to learn. We were also pretty clear that we needed to support our special education students so that they would be successful, but we didn't want to point out their needs or make them feel inadequate.

So we would offer choices along the lines of "101 Alternatives to the Book Report"; wide-open choices that really stretched the boundaries of what we were working on. I clearly remember teaching *To Kill a Mockingbird* and giving students project options that seemed great at the time. One choice was to add an epilogue to the novel, explaining what happened to Scout and the citizens of Maycomb. Another option was to draw a map of Maycomb County. They could also create a compilation of music that could be the "soundtrack" for the book. We designed these choices to appeal to a variety of learning styles and needs. The problem was that these options weren't necessarily linked to any clear learning goals. These options often varied in terms of the scope of work required, and kids tended not to make choices based on what they wanted to do, they made them based on what their friends were doing. Also, we were teaching ninth-grade ELA, and too often we offered kids choices that they could be successful with without ever reading the book carefully or writing much at all. It appears that Judy and I were somewhat oblivious to these issues at the time.

Eventually, however, I started to question this approach, even though it was widely celebrated as excellent teaching. What finally made me take notice was my gradebook. How was it possible for me to know if a kid who drew a map had learned to read or write any better as a result of our study together? What if a struggling writer decided on the epilogue and did a terrible job? After all, I hadn't taught anyone to write an epilogue, I'd just offered it as an option. Did it matter that they were just picking what their friends were doing? They seemed happy, but . . . Struggling through these questions caused the only argument Judy and I ever had.

Looking back, what we didn't understand was how to establish and maintain learning targets, while thoughtfully designing aligned, purposeful, differentiated activities that met the specific needs of specific kids. We hadn't yet developed the pre-assessment matrix you will see at the end of this chapter. Because we weren't using pre-assessment tools to determine what our students actually needed, we were "spray painting" the differentiation—coating the room with lots of choices and hoping that some of them were the things kids would want or need. We were differentiating by default, rather than by design.

Purposefully Meeting Students' Readiness Needs

Fast forward to today. I am helping English Language Arts teacher Jennifer Cropo plan for her summer school class. Jennifer knows that high school students end up in summer school for lots of reasons. Some students truly do have trouble making meaning from text—most of them can decode words, but they don't know how or what to think about while they read. Other students are actually excellent readers and have plenty of schema to bring to challenging reading, but they lack enthusiasm or stamina—they *can* read, but they don't.

In her first unit, Jennifer has chosen to have her students read and think about several excerpts from the book *Fugitive Pieces* by Canadian poet Anne Michaels. This lyrical text offers an engaging story—that of a child who narrowly escapes Nazi soldiers who kill his family—and a multilayered, poetic style that offers readers plenty to think about. Jennifer wants to introduce her students to the Read Like a Reader/Read Like a Writer strategy (see page 79). This multipurpose strategy pushes students to read closely, to think about a text in two ways, and to re-read multiple times. When reading like a reader, students consider the meaning of the text and focus on developing an understanding of it. When reading like a writer, however, students focus on what an author does to create text—the craft. They wonder about the choices an author made and focus closely on word choice, allusions, figurative language, parallel structure, and the like. Teachers might use the Read Like a Reader/Read Like a Writer strategy to help students meet targets such as "I can gather evidence from text to support my conclusion about what it means," or "I can determine the implicit message of literature," or "I can interpret words and phrases as they are used in text."

As Jennifer reflects on those targets, she has a hunch that her students are all over the place in relation to them. Some students actually know how to do these things, they just need to be continually nudged to practice with increasingly challenging texts. Some really don't know how—yet. Jennifer is thinking about three things: the students, the text, and the strategy she wants her students to use. When she is thinking about all three of these things, Jennifer is considering her students' reading *readiness,* rather than her students' reading *ability*. Reading ability is more of a static domain—we think about students as either "advanced," "grade-level," or "struggling" readers. When we consider students' *readiness* for a reading task, we think about them on a more fluid continuum; How ready *is* this kid for *this* task and *this* text, today?

Many factors play into students' reading readiness. One of those factors is, indeed, their reading ability. But other factors are also significant. Students with substantial background knowledge on a topic can read and comprehend texts on a much higher level than their reading ability might suggest. Students who are highly motivated to read something will read it and understand a great deal of it, regardless of their ability. Students who have completed a certain task many times don't have to give the pattern of that task a lot of brain space, which frees up their thinking for more challenging text. When differentiating to help students read challenging text, it's important to consider readiness.

Jennifer knows that it makes all kinds of sense to check in on her students' readiness for new strategies and new texts before she digs deeply into planning. Several weeks before she intends to actually begin the unit, Jennifer asks her students to complete a short pre-assessment. She briefly explains the Read Like a Reader/Read Like a Writer strategy and then asks students to give it a try. She doesn't do much modeling at this point because she wants to know what her students will do without her support. The goal, at this point, is for Jennifer to understand where her students stand in relation to this task and text. She understands that some students will need support going forward. She distributes the following handout:

Fugitive Pieces: Checking on This	Name _____	
Read Like a Writer		**Read Like a Reader**
Underline specific words and phrases you believe the author uses to make an impact on the reader. Once you have underlined, write about the things you chose. What impact do these things have on you?	My sister had long outgrown the hiding place. Bella was fifteen and even I admitted she was beautiful, with heavy brows and magnificent hair like black syrup, thick and luxurious, a muscle down her back. "A work of art," our mother said, brushing it for her while Bella sat in a chair. I was still small enough to vanish behind the wallpaper in the cupboard, cramming my head sideways between choking plaster and beams, eyelashes scraping. Since those minutes inside the wall, I've imagined that the dead lose every sense except hearing. The burst door.	Read the passage and then make an inference about what this text is about. Write your inference here:
	Wood ripped from hinges, cracking like ice under the shouts. Noises never heard before, torn from my father's mouth. Then silence. My mother had been sewing a button on my shirt. She kept her buttons in a chipped saucer. I heard the rim of the saucer in circles on the floor. I heard the spray of buttons, little white teeth.	Explain your inference with specific words and phrases from the text.
How comfortable are you with this strategy? Got it _____ Think I've got it Worried/don't get it		
How comfortable are you with this text? I understand it I think I understand it ????		

As Jennifer examines her students' work on the "Checking on This" handout, she finds some of what she expected, as well as a few surprises. Almost all of her students got a sense of violence from the excerpt. About half of the students could provide specifics to back up that sense—Bella hiding, the door being ripped from hinges, the connection between the buttons and teeth. Certain kids who she thought would find the text super challenging did (they freely circled "????"), and certain kids who she thought would be confident with the strategy were. But she also found that a few students who she expected would struggle really didn't, and that others who she thought would fly were faltering a bit.

Purposeful Pre-assessment

Jennifer took a really important step in terms of purposeful differentiation. She established clarity about what she wanted her students to be able to do and developed learning targets to guide the work. Then she used pre-assessment to more closely determine who could do it and who couldn't do it quite yet—their readiness. This step, what I call "pre-assessment with a goal in mind," is essential in terms of making differentiation that makes a difference. Without pre-assessment, how can teachers be sure of which students need what?

Pre-assessment can be done in a number of ways. It's important to know, first, what you are pre-assessing *for*, which takes us right back to the use of learning targets. When a learning target is knowledge-based, then the pre-assessment should be knowledge-based. For example, a social studies teacher might wonder how much background knowledge his students have about the Civil War. Actual knowledge about the events leading up to the Civil War, the main conflicts and where they occurred, and key decisions made by military leaders are all learning targets in his Civil War unit. In this case, a simple check-in quiz could work, where the teacher asks direct questions about these things to find out what the students already know and don't know.

However, pre-assessments for *skills* and *reasoning,* which most reading learning targets would reflect, are another matter altogether. Let's say the same social studies teacher, above, is also planning to use primary source documents in his unit. If he is planning to help all of his students meet the challenge of complex text, he needs to know which of his students can already read and think about primary source documents well—their readiness for primary sources—and which of his students find it challenging. In determining the answer to that question, he needs to consider the following variables:

> What are my students' general reading levels? Do I have data that helps me understand, specifically, which kids are reading below grade level and which are reading at and above grade level? What predictions can I make from that data about how my students will do with primary sources?

> Since reading primary source documents is a specific skill within the larger context of reading, do I know, specifically, how my students already do with primary sources? Have I asked them to read enough primary sources that I know who does well with them and who doesn't, despite their overall reading skill? If not, can I have them read one now and then take a look?

> Am I planning to introduce a new strategy related to primary sources? If so, how can I check to see if they understand it before I assign more work with that strategy? (This is what English teacher Jennifer Cropo did when she checked in on her students' fluency and comfort with the Read Like a Read/Read Like a Writer strategy and the first chunk of text from *Fugitive Pieces.*)

When Judy and I were first teaching our integrated class, we only knew about students' general reading skill, which is one of the factors that led us to such broad, and somewhat sloppy, differentiation. Because we knew only that we had "high," "regular," and "low" readers, we didn't think enough about what we should be doing to differentiate within specific genres, or which kids needed what when it came to specific strategies—their readiness. We needed to do more of the kind of pre-assessment that Jennifer did—to ask: how are kids doing with *this* text and *this* strategy, *today*?

An Essential Approach: Tiered Processing Activities

In the last chapter, we learned that teaching complex texts involves strategizing to create a "prepare-process-assess" paradigm, and that the process phase of complex text–based lessons could include differentiated processing activities. Because Jennifer designed a pre-assessment that was aligned with her learning targets, she was able to design purposeful differentiated processing activities as her next step. She created two versions of the next Read Like a Reader/Read Like a Writer activity that she wanted her students to complete. The first version, below, is highly scaffolded to help students read the challenging text. It directs students where to pay close attention to the text so that they discover specific details that will help them develop a deeper understanding of it as a whole.

Fugitive Pieces: Introduction	Name _____	
Read Like a Writer		**Read Like a Reader**
Can you associate this imagery with any specific ethnic group?	My sister had long outgrown the hiding place. Bella was fifteen and even I admitted she was beautiful, with heavy brows and magnificent hair like black syrup, thick and luxurious, a muscle down her back. "A work of art," our mother said, brushing it for her while Bella sat in a chair. I was still small enough to vanish behind the wallpaper in the cupboard, cramming my head sideways between choking plaster and beams, eyelashes scraping.	Why might this family have a hiding place?
Think about the word *spray* and the comparison of buttons to teeth. What reasons would the author have for this word choice?	Since those minutes inside the wall, I've imagined that the dead lose every sense except hearing. The burst door. Wood ripped from hinges, cracking like ice under the shouts. Noises never heard before, torn from my father's mouth. Then silence. My mother had been sewing a button on my shirt. She kept her buttons in a chipped saucer. I heard the rim of the saucer in circles on the floor. I heard the spray of buttons, little white teeth.	What reasons might there be for the boy to associate being inside the wall to being dead? What is your inference about what has happened to this family?
Think about it…let's discuss. Did focusing on a few specific points in the text deepen your understanding as a whole? What did you notice about the places I asked you to look deeper?		

Notice the scaffolding Jennifer provided. She pointed out Bella's description and prompted the readers to think about her ethnicity without saying "Bella is Jewish, and this story is set in Nazi-occupied Poland," which would pretty much negate the students' need to read deeply and think critically. Jennifer drew attention to "hiding," which triggered background knowledge important for understanding the text, but that still made it necessary for her students to read and think. She had the students pause after revisiting this text, both to think about deeper reading and what they came to understand about the text as a result. These kinds of scaffolds are important in helping all students read complex texts. They support the students in doing the work, but they don't exempt students from doing the work.

Other students showed through the pre-assessment that they did not need the amount of scaffolding that is provided in the previous example. The text and task were just right for them; they showed that they could likely keep going in a more independent fashion. So Jennifer created another version of the activity for them, shown below.

Fugitive Pieces: Introduction Name _____		
Read Like a Writer		**Read Like a Reader**
	My sister had long outgrown the hiding place. Bella was fifteen and even I admitted she was beautiful, with heavy brows and magnificent hair like black syrup, thick and luxurious, a muscle down her back. "A work of art," our mother said, brushing it for her while Bella sat in a chair. I was still small enough to vanish behind the wallpaper in the cupboard, cramming my head sideways between choking plaster and beams, eyelashes scraping.	
	Since those minutes inside the wall, I've imagined that the dead lose every sense except hearing. The burst door. Wood ripped from hinges, cracking like ice under the shouts. Noises never heard before, torn from my father's mouth. Then silence. My mother had been sewing a button on my shirt. She kept her buttons in a chipped saucer. I heard the rim of the saucer in circles on the floor. I heard the spray of buttons, little white teeth.	
	Blackness filled me, spread from the back of my head into my eyes as if my brain had been punctured. Spread from stomach to legs. I gulped and gulped, swallowing it whole. The wall filled with smoke. I struggled out and stared while the air caught fire.	
	I wanted to go to my parents, to touch them. But I couldn't, unless I stepped on their blood.	
	The soul leaves the body instantly, as if it can hardly wait to be free: my mother's face was not her own. My father was twisted with falling. Two shapes in the flesh-heap, his hands.	

Although the second version is less scaffolded, it still involves a strategy that requires students to read the text several times and to notice and note what they are reading and thinking. It requires them to do so without the scaffold of the strategic questions. Jennifer's purposeful differentiation, called a tiered activity, is targeted to give students the practice they specifically need to develop their skill and confidence with complex text. When Jennifer's students worked on these activities, they were all meeting the same Common Core–based learning targets: "I can gather evidence from text to support my conclusion about what it means," or "I can determine the implicit message of literature," or "I can interpret words and phrases as they are used in text." Some students met those targets with scaffolding and some met them without. Jennifer's goal, as she works her way through the excerpts with her class, is to remove the scaffolding for students who no longer need it, to move them from the scaffolded version of the activity to the unscaffolded version.

Tiered activities are based on psychologist Lev Vygotsky's theory of the "zone of proximal development" (ZPD). The zone of proximal development is the space in which a student is being asked to practice a skill that's just slightly beyond what he or she already knows how to do. It's easy to see this theory in practice when we watch kids improving their skill in sports, say, or when mastering a video game. They try, get lots of feedback, learn more, try again, get lots of feedback, and learn more. There's a sense that they are improving and pushing forward. It's in this zone where learning occurs. Elementary school teachers who routinely teach students how to read are very familiar with the zone of proximal development; they coach students through several texts at a certain level, and then ascertain whether or not those students are ready for the next level, and if so, move them on.

Offering increasingly challenging texts, as elementary school teachers do, is one way to improve older students' reading skill. But another way, and perhaps sometimes a better way, is to fit the *task* we ask students to accomplish with a text into their zones of proximal development. Jennifer did this for her summer school class by providing one scaffolded task for the readers who needed it and a less scaffolded version for the others. Jennifer's scaffolds for all students included:

> - The Read Like a Reader/Read Like a Writer strategy. As is discussed in Chapter 4, strategies that cause students to "work" a text, rather than questions that only measure students' understanding of a text, increase comprehension.

> - Asking students to read the same text more than one time.

> - Providing the text on the handout, so that students can write on/annotate the text.

Jennifer's scaffolding increased for the more challenged readers:

> › Directing students to read specific lines closely.

> › Directing students to notice key vocabulary.

> › Surfacing helpful background knowledge.

Other important scaffolds that teachers might offer readers grappling with a challenging text are:

> › Reading and re-reading shorter pieces, or breaking longer text into chunks.

> › Providing structured discussion activities that prompt students to return to the text for evidence.

> › Matching graphic organizers with the pattern of text. For example, if the text is organized in a main-idea-and-supporting-details format, the graphic organizer that less-ready readers are using should reflect the same pattern. More-ready readers can work between and among text formats.

> › Adding illustrations or pairing challenging texts with helpful pictures/visuals.

> › Word banks or glossaries specific to the text.

> › Direct instruction of vocabulary that is essential to understanding the text or task. In the *Fugitive Pieces* activity, the word "imagery"—a task word—is essential. There isn't a word in the text that would stop a reader from getting the point.

> › More time, especially time spent in a structured reading/thinking activity.

Providing specific scaffolds for the readers who need it, or tiering activities, as Jennifer is doing, is part of the planning challenge, and this does, indeed, take time. But when we choose to avoid this work by withholding challenging text from older students, we are withholding access to rich vocabulary and background knowledge that's going to help our students read other challenging texts.

Most adults confront challenging text every day—no one says, "Here's an easier version of our company's insurance policy overview if you need it." Adult readers create their own scaffolds if they need them—they ask questions, they look up additional background information, they make notes, etc. Our goal in differentiating for older students should be to build confidence in them that they can deal with difficult reading. Offering them challenging reading, with support, is the first step in that process.

The Power of Choice

Judy and I might have been misguided in our implementation of choice and learning preference–based differentiation, but we weren't wrong about its value in the classroom. Choice matters, and it matters especially to adolescents. The key to making choice worthwhile is limited, well-structured choices that enable students to meet essential learning targets.

When I was teaching, I loved helping students grapple with *Romeo and Juliet*. Many teachers differentiate Shakespeare by offering different "translations" of the play, even comic-book versions. To me, that's a scenario just begging for some target clarity. If the primary purpose of reading Shakespeare is just to know the plot of his plays, then it's true that comic-book versions could get the job done. But if the target is to help students understand Shakespeare's particular genius with language and wordplay, then reading versions close to the original is important. Sure, the language is hard, but my experience is that students are very motivated to tackle it. When you have that kind of motivation going for you, definitely capitalize on it by ensuring that all students work with the same challenging, central text. Now is the time to differentiate by interest and learning preference, rather than by readiness.

I warmed up my students for *Romeo and Juliet* by having them complete short research projects to familiarize themselves with the context for Shakespeare's work—Elizabethan times. I wanted my students to understand the original audiences for his work—a broad swath of English society. I learned pretty quickly, though, that offering wide-open choice to students, as is "research any lifestyle from Elizabethan times," frequently ended in disaster, as the most appropriate resources were not necessarily available. In addition, I found myself frantic as I tried to support a diverse group of students researching too wide of a variety of topics.

So I learned to bring some structure to this kind of differentiation by using a technique that goes by several names—choice boards, menus, or contracts. All of these structures have to do with students making a choice and agreeing to certain conditions, usually relating to deadlines, essential components, and working conditions. An example from my *Romeo and Juliet* research project follows on the next page

Notice how in this experience, even though the students are choosing different activities and roles to research, they will all be meeting the same target. I call this type of menu "managed choice." You get kids' input into the work they want to complete, but by having them rank order, you maintain some control over which kids actually end up doing what work. When I chose not to give students their first choice on any particular work (if, for example, I thought they picked something as their first choice just because their friends did), I would strive to give them their first choice for the next project.

Rank-Order Your Lifestyle Choice: Living in Shakespeare's World

Learning Target: I can research to describe the lifestyle of a member of Elizabethan society.

Your task is to gather and synthesize key information about life in or near London during Shakespeare's time in order to understand the audience he was initially entertaining with his plays. You will fulfill this task by taking on the perspective of a certain member of English society—a knight, merchant, nobleman or woman, monk or nun, craftsman, artist/playwright, scholar, or peasant—and then completing a team project with students who have chosen other perspectives.

Use the rank-order slip below to let me know which lifestyle you are interested in researching.

Once your choice has been determined, you will research these subtopics:

► Basic Needs—What do you eat and wear? What kind of home do you have?

► Economics—How do you get your money, and how does that shape your life?

► Work/Responsibilities—How do you spend your time?

► Education—What education is available to you, and how does that impact you?

► Religion—What do you believe? How do those beliefs affect the choices you make?

► Entertainment at the Globe Theater—What would a visit to the Globe be like for you? Where would you sit/stand? How would you behave?

You will use books, encyclopedias, other reference materials, and the Internet to find your information. Record your research on notecards or in a graphic organizer, whichever works best for you. Be sure to keep track of your sources.

Complete the form below in order to let me know the lifestyle you would like to research.

Name _____

Put a "1" on the line for your first choice, "2" for your second, and "3" for your third.

____ knight	____ craftsman
____ merchant	____ artist/playwright
____ nobleman or woman	____ scholar
____ monk or nun	____ peasant

Contracts and menus are not meant to be distributed instead of teaching—worst-case scenario is handing out the menu above and then setting kids free for a couple of weeks to get the work done. Contracts and menus give shape and clarity of content to several periods of a class in which the teacher provides minilessons (in this case, on the structure and close reading of free verse), and then opens up space and time for kids to work independently or in small groups with additional processing strategies, to conference with the teacher to get feedback on their reading or writing, and to revise and edit their work. In fact, the particular menu on the previous page was used as part of a two-week unit in which the students were guided through several stages of the research process. I used the following pre-assessment to help me understand what support students needed as they worked through the research I required:

Name _____

Research Pre-assessment

Check your level of expertise/comfort with each of the research and library targets listed below. Your input will help me plan to support you (or stay out of your way) as we work together in the library over the next couple of weeks.

Target	No Brainer	Slightly Challenging	Kind of Hard	Help, I'm Drowning!
I can use the Internet to find specific information.				
I can use books or reference materials to find specific information.				
I can read and understand informational text.				
When I am taking notes, I can determine what details are important to capture.				
I can take notes in a way that helps me synthesize ideas.				
I can stay focused when many others are talking or moving around.				
Other—write in anything you think I've forgotten: _____				

You can likely imagine how students' responses on the pre-assessment shaped the mini-lessons I developed and how I worked with students over the next couple of weeks. Because so many students were confident that they had mastered the Internet, the librarian and I developed an additional pre-assessment in which students had to research a couple of things and then describe how they found the information. Any student who "passed" that pre-assessment was allowed to opt out of the whole-class lesson regarding the use of search engines and databases. We realized that we needed to have a whole-class lesson about using indexes in books, and we also coached individual students once they got started. The librarian arranged some inter-library loans to have materials available for a wide range of readability, and I spent time with a small group of students, previewing materials to help them find the resources they needed. We set up "quiet areas," and I approached and reminded specific students about using them, based on what they had indicated on their pre-assessment. This "double differentiation"—choice, plus needed support—set up many students for success. What I mostly noticed when I took this approach was *engagement*. What you see in classrooms where teachers offer choice plus support is more kids working more of the time.

Choice by Learning Preference

Another basis for choice is to design reading tasks based on students' learning preferences. Learning preferences are what make a learner a learner—culture, attitudes, competencies, styles, gender, and interests. Many teachers are familiar with the work of Howard Gardner, whose work reflects humans' differing capacities for processing several kinds of information and various interests in different disciplines. He calls these differing capacities and interests "intelligences," and as of this writing, he has named nine intelligences. Learning styles, on the other hand, have more to do with a person's various approaches to, or ways of, learning, such as if a person more readily receives new information by hearing it, seeing it, or touching it, or by all of the variety of combinations there could be.

As a high school English teacher, I struggled to support my students' various learning preferences. After all, I was teaching them a fairly narrow, albeit important, thing amongst the scope of all there is to learn in the world. Literacy, by its very nature, definitely favors visual and auditory learners who have a preference for verbal-linguistic approaches. I could make a case for some kinesthetic approaches when I was teaching, especially when we were studying dramas, but my kids couldn't really act out their research papers or design mathematical formulas to explain characters' motivations. (On second thought, maybe some of them could do that, but I sure didn't know how to evaluate it!) In fact, it was when I forgot to focus on literacy development that I spun off into choices that didn't make as much sense, such as assigning the map of Maycomb County versus the epilogue of *To Kill a Mockingbird*.

Then I learned about the work of Robert Sternberg, a cognitive psychologist, who defines his approach to learning preferences as "thinking styles." Sternberg posits that intelligence is triarchic—meaning that there are three aspects to it—the capacity to think creatively, practically, and analytically. People have all three intelligences, Sternberg says, but some might have stronger preferences in one realm or another. Success comes in balancing the three, or in finding contexts in which the particular preference(s) a person has are valued.

Learners with analytic preferences have "schoolhouse smarts." These encompass the ability to analyze, compare and contrast, and evaluate information. Analytic learners in the literacy-based classroom like comparing and contrasting characters and texts, they like rubrics and applying them, they like Socratic seminars and other experiences where they can use logic and evidence to pursue an argument.

People with practical preferences have "street smarts." These involve the capacity to apply what is learned, particularly in real-world contexts. Practical learners in the classroom like to know the "why" of what they are doing and sometimes don't get the idea of learning just for the sake of learning. They are also often natural leaders and are drawn to helping people solve problems. They might be inspired by the compelling or localized context as described in Chapter 2.

Learners with creative preferences enjoy theorizing. They like coming up with new ideas, thinking of novel scenarios, and supposing things are different. They often enjoy acting in plays and learning through "make-believe." Creative learners enjoy composing, writing, and drawing and are successful in the literacy-based classroom when there are opportunities to model work after real-world authors, to think outside the box and create new forms, and to think beyond the story as to what characters might do or say in other settings.

Sternberg's research shows that students benefit from sometimes having the opportunity to learn and think in all three ways, and that they sometimes benefit from working to their strengths. In fact, he found that students who are taught with a focus on all three kinds of thinking achieve more, even when learning is measured by analytic means, such as on standardized tests.

What I like most about applying Sternberg's work to the classroom is that it helps me think about shaping the three types of reading- and writing-based tasks (analytic, creative, and practical), all of which can be focused on the same learning targets. You might have noticed that students were not tasked with writing a research paper in their "choose an Elizabethan lifestyle" project. That's because there was a second phase to that project, a learning profile–based choice. The second choice students made in that project follows on the next page.

The first choice, the dialogue, falls into the "creative" realm. The second choice reflects the work of real museum curators and so is a more "practical" option. The third choice, a

Rank-Order Your Project Choice #2: Living in Shakespeare's World

Learning Target: I can synthesize my information with others' to develop a deeper understanding of life during Elizabethan times.

After we have completed the research phase of this project, I will put you in a group with 2–3 other students. The purpose of these teams is for you to share the information you have learned with others, for them to share with you, and for all of you to bring your information together in an interesting way. As a team, you will complete one of the following:

▶ Imagine that the members of your team met while waiting in line outside of the Globe Theater. Write the dialogue that would result from this encounter. Your dialogue should reveal several key aspects of each of your lives, as well as your attitude and expectations about seeing the play. Rehearse your dialogue and be prepared to perform it for others.

▶ Imagine that you are historians working at a museum. You have been charged with creating a display that compares and contrasts the lives of different people who lived during the Elizabethan era, specifically in or near London. The museum display should include artifacts—physical objects that are important to each of your perspectives (these can be symbolic rather than actual artifacts, of course)—as well as pictures and display notes. At least part of your display should show how the members of your team feel about Shakespeare and/or the Globe Theater. Be sure to show and explain how the lives of the people you have researched are similar and different.

▶ Work together to make two charts. One should show the advantages and disadvantages of living in or near London during Elizabethan times. Be sure that this chart includes both advantages and disadvantages from each of your researched perspectives and that it incorporates information about the Globe. The second chart should show both the advantages and disadvantages of being a teenager in modern times, including entertainments of your choice. After the collaborative charts are done, each member of the team should write an essay comparing and contrasting Elizabethan life and modern life. Although these essays will contain common ideas, they should be completed individually.

Name _____

Put a "1" on the line of your first choice, "2" on your second choice, and "3" on your last choice.

_____ Dialogue   _____ Museum Display   _____ Charts fairly traditional school task, is "analytical." I always loved the creative tasks, but plenty of my students chose the other options, always perceiving the others to be "more work." Just as during the reading/research phase of this project, students were supported as needed during the writing phase of this project through targeted minilessons, conferences, and feedback.

Purposeful differentiation holds all students accountable for completing fairly equal amounts of rigorous work. A good check to see if you are on the right track with that is seeing if you can design a rubric that guides students' work no matter which choice they make. For example, I used the following rubric to help clarify my expectations on the Living in Shakespeare's World final products:

Rubric for Living in Shakespeare's World Projects			
Criteria	**3**	**2**	**1**
Content of the Project	The project provides ample detailed, accurate information about all of the lifestyles represented in your group. The viewer/reader obtains both information and insight into the way people lived during Shakespeare's time. You have integrated your individual work into a seamless whole. The participants' perspectives on the Globe Theater are clearly represented.	The project provides accurate information about all of the lifestyles represented in your group, but there are gaps in the information expected and that which is included. The viewer/reader still has questions about the way people lived during Shakespeare's time and/or about how participants felt about the Globe Theater. Work from all members of your group is included, but the individual parts are not integrated.	There are many gaps in the information expected and that which is included. The viewer/reader does not learn about the way people lived during Shakespeare's time and/or about how participants felt about the Globe Theater. Some members of the group did not contribute.
Quality of the Project	Your group used your time and resources wisely. Your project shows attention to detail, care, and a desire to achieve. The written portions of your project have been edited and follow the conventions of standard written English.	Your group needed to be reminded to use your time and resources wisely. Your project lacks finishing touches; its appearance is merely adequate. The written portions of your project contain many errors.	Despite several warnings, your group did not use the time and/or resources wisely. Your project is sloppy or incomplete. There are so many errors in your written work that it's hard to understand.

Rather than "spray painting" learning preference–based differentiation, smart teachers use it purposefully—to provide motivating choices to their learners while maintaining high expectations for literacy development. Approaches like this are the very important middle ground in which teachers can still respond to the needs of their students while staying focused on a rigorous curriculum.

I'd like to make a final important point about the research unit leading up to *Romeo and Juliet*. I needed to have the whole thing carefully planned, starting with a targets-assessment chart, prior to starting the unit with students. The relationship between students choosing which Elizabethan lifestyle to research, the actual research process, and the development of their final products was so interrelated, there was no way to actually get to where we wanted to go without knowing the end point before we began. Beginning with the end in mind also helped me envision the potential areas for differentiation and design the pre-assessments. As discussed in Chapter 3, a targets-assessments chart can help teachers stay true to where they need to go. Adding a possible differentiation column to the chart provides a quick overview of potential areas for differentiation and the kinds of pre-assessment needed. The pre-assessment matrix for the first part of the Living in Shakespeare's World unit looked like this:

Long-Term Target: I can research to describe the lifestyle of a member of Elizabethan society.		
Supporting Targets	**Assessment(s)**	**Possible Differentiation and Pre-assessment Needed**
I can use the Internet to find specific information.	Notes from Internet sources	Some students need a search-engine review? Do they all? Check on this.
I can use books or reference materials to find specific information.	Notes from books and reference materials	How fluent are students with indexes? Check on this.
I can read and understand informational text.	Notes from a variety of sources	I know I have some students reading well below grade level. I should offer a wide variety of resources and also work with a small group—more of a guided close-reading approach—perhaps limiting their sources and providing cloze notes.
When I am taking notes, I can determine what details are important to capture.	Check students' notes for relevancy	Conference with students on this as they are working. Small-group instruction, if needed.
I can organize notes in a way that helps me synthesize ideas.	List-Group-Label strategy (see page 102). Review students' groupings prior to starting part two of the project.	Tier the List-Group-Label activity by providing some students with the labels. Small-group instruction, if needed.

It's Planning Time Spent Now or Later

Many teachers have remarked to me that this part of planning—proactively planning to differentiate the processing activities—in order to meet the challenge of teaching students to more effectively read complex text is the part of planning that they don't have time to do. Research shows that this is a common response, particularly when it comes to meeting the needs of exceptional children (Schumm et al. 1995).

It's not that teachers don't care about their students with exceptionalities; in fact, research shows that they are very likely to take steps to help their students adjust, socially and emotionally, to the general education setting and to be accepted by their peers. But ". . . even teachers who were identified as being effective in working with students with learning disabilities did not preplan specifically for the students with learning disabilities. Many teachers planned for diversity in their classrooms by structuring multifaceted activities that encouraged the involvement of all students (this was less true of secondary teachers than elementary). As one teacher put it, 'Students need to go with the stream; the stream will not change for them.'" (Schumm et al. 1995).

According to this research, teachers, particularly secondary teachers, noted that they felt sure there were plenty of supports in place for students in their classes who did not "get it" to get help (study hall, resource room, after school, etc.). But additional research shows that students with disabilities rarely ask for such support from teachers or even peers (McIntosh et al. 1994).

I point this out because it reveals an important cost of not planning thoroughly to meet the needs of a variety of students. Expecting the system to "react" to students' needs isn't effective, and it is expensive in terms of time, resources, and emotions. I have known plenty of teachers to give up the planning time they have embedded in their workdays to help struggling students. But this help often looks like re-explaining the same ideas and material that happened in class. Furthermore, it puts the teacher behind the eight ball in terms of planning for what is to happen the next day—another fuzzy lesson, another set of students wondering why they can't seem to understand. Better planning can lead to increased student engagement and achievement the first time through, actually freeing up teacher time that's currently spent remediating students.

When I was teaching, our district allowed—and in fact encouraged—Judy and me to think about how best to use substitute teachers to free us up for planning well together. I know there's a gut-level reaction to that idea among teachers, typically along the lines of "I can't afford more time out of my classroom!" But when Judy and I looked carefully at our schedules, we realized that there were opportunities to plan together that were low-impact on our students. We didn't always need to be present when students were taking tests, for example. Some days, because of special events at the school, our class periods had already been shortened so much that a really rich class period wasn't possible. We learned to use those days for planning, and it helped us stay ahead of the curve (if only we'd known what we were doing it would have been really excellent!) The bottom line is that planning to proactively and thoughtfully differentiate lessons involving complex text is an investment that pays off for students *and* teachers.

Keys to Help You Make This Critical Move

To recap, purposeful differentiation to help students meet the challenge of complex text involves:

> starting from clear, standards-based, learning targets

> pre-assessing to see where students are in relation to these targets

> sometimes planning specific scaffolded and less scaffolded processing activities, based on students' reading readiness

> removing supports, as needed, over time

> sometimes offering interest or learning preference–based choices that are tightly aligned to learning targets

> finding the time to do this proactively, rather than reactively.

Works Cited

McIntosh, R., Sharon Vaughn, Jeanne Shay Schumm, Diane Haager, and Lee, O. 1994. Observations of students with learning disabilities in general education classrooms. *Exceptional Children,* 60(3): 249–261.

Schumm, Jeanne Shay, Sharon Vaughn, Diane Haager, Judith McDowell, et al. 1995. General education teacher planning: What can students with learning disabilities expect? *Exceptional Children,* 61 (February): 335.

Sternberg, Robert. 1999. *Thinking Styles.* Cambridge University Press.

— PARTING THOUGHTS —

Many people perceive teaching to be the thing that's happening when the teacher and students are in the room together. But teachers know that the quality of the work that happens with learners is directly impacted by the quality of the work that happens when the learners aren't present. High-quality, standards-aligned planning leads to more kids learning what they need to be learning, more of the time.

I challenge you, in this time of tremendous possibility, to increase the rigor of your daily practice through thoughtful planning. Find time to talk with your colleagues about the possibilities for your teaching. Write down your ideas, and firm them up in such a way as to literally publish your own Common Core–aligned units. Dream. Think outside the box about your content and what it could mean to your students if it's wrapped in a compelling context. Read.

Think differently about how you and your students spend time together. Talk less, so there is room for *them* to read and think and talk and do. Give your learners the gift of struggle. Teach them to persist. Care about them enough to demand that they try.

Eleanor Roosevelt is widely credited with saying, "It takes as much energy to wish as it does to plan." With all due respect to Mrs. Roosevelt, I don't believe that's really true. It takes more energy to plan, it does. But without plans, our wishes for our students to become better readers, our wishes for them to become more independent critical thinkers, and our wishes for them to be college and career ready by the time they graduate high school will remain just that—wishes.

Make plans.